Geography Matters 2

HIGHER

Series Editor:

John Hopkin

Authors:

Nicola Arber, Bournville School, Birmingham

Heather Blades, Deepings School, Peterborough

Lisa James, Cockshut Hill School, Birmingham

Sue Lomas, Henbury High School, Macclesfield

Garrett Nagle, St Edward's School, Oxford

Chris Ryan, formerly at Heston Community School, London

Linda Thompson, formerly at Sandbach School, Sandbach

Paul Thompson, Ounsdale High School, Wolverhampton

Heinemann

Heinemann is an imprint of Pearson Education Limited, a company incorporated in England and Wales, having its registered office at Edinburgh Gate, Harlow, Essex, CM20 2JE.
Registered company number: 872828
Heinemann is a registered trademark of Pearson Education Limited

First published 2001

ISBN: 978 0 435355 17 3

12

12

Designed and illustrated by Gecko Ltd, Bicester, Oxon, Dave Mostyn and Peter Bull
Original illustrations © Heinemann Educational Publishers 2001
Printed in China (CTPS/12)

Acknowledgements

The authors and publishers would like to thank the following for permission to use copyright material.

Maps and extracts

p.6 Alan Bilham-Boult, People, Places & Themes / ; **p.8 A, 9 B** Maps reproduced from Ordnance Survey maps with the permission of the Controller of Her Majesty's Stationary Office © Crown Copyright; License No. 398020; **p.14 E** Maps reproduced from Ordnance Survey maps with the permission of the Controller of Her Majesty's Stationary Office © Crown Copyright; License No. 398020; **p.26 A** Maps reproduced from Ordnance Survey maps with the permission of the Controller of Her Majesty's Stationary Office © Crown Copyright; License No. 398020; **p.27** www.BBC.co.uk; **p.29, 31, 36 A** Maps reproduced from Ordnance Survey maps with the permission of the Controller of Her Majesty's Stationary Office © Crown Copyright; License No. 398020; **p.47** Philips Modern School Atlas / George Philip Ltd; **p.51** Philips Children's Atlas / George Philips; **p.54** www.bbc.co.uk/weather/worldweather/europe/index; **p.57 F** Philips Foundation Atlas / George Philips; **p.59 B, C** Waugh, The UK and Europe / **p.68 C** Philips Atlas / George Philips; **p.69 A** Attica Interactive 1997; **p.69 B** Philips Atlas / George Philips; **p.90 A** Philips Atlas / George Philips; **p.91 C** Collins Longman Student Atlas; **p.97 B** Tony Waltham, Karst and Caves / Yorkshire Dales National Park and the British Cave Research Association; **p.98 D, 99 G, 101 J** Maps reproduced from Ordnance Survey maps with the permission of the Controller of Her Majesty's Stationary Office © Crown Copyright; License No. 398020; **p.108 A** Philips University Atlas / George Philips; **p.120 B** Understanding Global Issues – World Fishing; **p.122 B, 123 D** www.guardianunlimited.co.uk ; **p.136 A, B, 137 C, D** www.thamesvalley.police.uk .

Photographs

4 A Stock Market/Tibor Bognar; **4 B** SPL/Earth Satellite Corp.; **4 C** Corbis / Robert Holmes; **4 D** Mike Ridout; **4 E** FLPA/Fritz Pölking; **5 F** FLPA/Robin Chittenden; **5 G** PA Photos / Owen Humphreys; **5 H** Stock Market; **5 I** Stock Market; **5 J** Stock Market/John M. Roberts; **6 A** Alan Bilham-Boult; **6 B** Alan Bilham-Boult; **6 C** David Tarn; **7 D** FLPA/Mike J. Thomas; **10** Heather Blades; **11 A** Collections/John & Eliza Forder; **18** PA Photos/John Giles; **19 B** John Hopkin; **19 C** John Hopkin; **20 A** FLPA/Mike J Thomas; **20 B** Stock Market/Jose Fuste Rago; **20 C** Stock Market; **20 D** Stock Market/T Stewart; **20 E** FLPA/P. Moore; **22 A** David Tarn; **22 B** Stock Market; **22 C** FLPA/Peter Reynolds; **22 D** Corbis/John Farmer/Cordaiy PL; **22 E** Sue Lomas; **23 B** Sue Lomas; **24 E** Sue Lomas; **27** Camera Press/Andrew Hasson; **28 A** John Connors Press Associates; PA Photos/Tim Ockenden; **30** Katz Pictures; **32 A** Stock Market; **32 B** Courtesy USGS; **33 A** Stock Market; **33 B** Stock Market; **34 A** Stock Market; **34 B** Sue Cunningham; **34 C** The Trafford Centre; **34 D** Stock Market; **34 E** Stock Market; **34 F** Stock Market; **35 G** (l-r) Stock Market; Stock Market/Matthias Kulka; Stock Market; Stock Market/Rob Lewine; Barry Atkinson; Peter Morris; Chris Honeywell; Rupert Horrox; Stock Market/Steve Prezant; Rupert Horrox; Hemera Photo-Objects; Gareth Boden; **36 B** Nicola Arber; **37 C** John Hopkin; **37 D** John Hopkin; **37 E** Nicola Arber; **40 A** Stock Market; **40 B** Collections/Liz Stares; **40 D** Stock Market/Charles Gupton; **41** Joan Davies; Joan Davies; **46** University of Dundee; **48 A** Corbis/ Richard Hamilton Smith; **48 B** Stock Market; **48 C** Stock Market; **51 D** University of Dundee; **52 A** University of Dundee; **52 B** Jeremy Krause; **52 D** University of Dundee; **52 E** Jeremy Krause; **52 G** University of Dundee; **52 H** Jeremy Krause; **61 D** John Hopkin; **62** (l-r) Stock Market; Associated Press/Fredrik Funck; James Davis Travel Photography; Corbis/Carl Purcell; Stock Market; FLPA/Mark Newman; **63 C** Stock Market; **63 E** PA Photos/John Giles; **63 F** BBC; **64 A** Corbis / Robert Holmes; **64 B** Sue Cunningham; **65 C** Stock Market; **66 E** Sue Cunningham; **66 F** Sue Cunningham; **67 G** Science Photo Library/Tom van Sant, Geosphere Project/Planetary Visions; **70 A** Sue Cunningham; **70 C** Sue Cunningham; **72 E** Sue Cunningham; **72 F** Sue Cunningham/Patrick Cunningham; **73 H** Sue Cunningham; **74 J** Oxford Scientific Films/George Bernard; **80 A** Sue Cunningham; Sue Cunningham; **83 E** SPL/NASA; **84 G** Sue Cunningham; **88 A** FLPA/W. Broadhurst; **88 B** John Hopkin; **88** David Tarn; **88 D** Camera Press/Colin Davey; **89 F** Sam Smith; **89 G** Stock Market; **89 H** FLPA/Keith Rushforth; **89 I** Stock Market; **93 D** SPL/Jon Wilson; **93 E** John Hopkin; **94 B** Sam Smith; **95 C** Sam Smith; **95 D** Corbis/Annie Griffiths Belt; **96 F** David Tarn; **96 G** Sam Smith; **96 H** David Tarn; **97 C** David Tarn; **99 F** David Tarn; **100 H** Lisa James; **103 M** David Tarn; **103 N** Stock Market; **104 left** Corbis/James Skok; **104 right** FLPA/Anthony T. Matthews; **106 A** Corbis / Lawson Wood; **106 B** David Tarn; **106 C** FLPA/Derek Hall; **106 D** PA Photos / EPA; **106 E** Oxford Scientific Films/Steve Turner; **110 B** Sue Cunningham; **111 D** Rex Features/SIPA; **113 D** Oxford Scientific Films/ Michael and Patricia Fogden; **113 E** Oxford Scientific Films/Tim Jackson; **113 F** FLPA/W Wisniewski; **113 G** FLPA/W Wisniewski; **113 H** Garden Matters; **116 A** David Tarn; **116 B** FLPA/S Jonasson; **116 C** Corbis / Reuters NewMedia Inc; **116 D** FLPA/Martin Smith; **117 E** Eye Ubiquitous/Lawson Wood; **117 F** Oxford Scientific Films/Doug Allan; **121 D** Eye Ubiquitous/Damian Peters; **121 E** Corbis / Natalie Fobes; **121 F** Corbis / Paul A. Souders; **124 A** Oxford Scientific Films/Scott Winer; **124 B** FLPA/Silvestria; **124 C** FLPA/Minden Pictures; **130 A** Associated Press/Dave Thomson; **130 B** Ronald Grant; **130 C** Associated Press/Itsu Inouye; **130 D** Camera Press/Gus Coral; **130 E, 134 A, 134 B, 134 C, 134 D, 134 E, 134 F, 134 G, 138 F, 138 I** Garrett Nagle.

Throughout the book these symbols are used with activities that use literacy, numeracy, science and ICT skills.

Contents

Websites: On pages where you are asked to go to www.heinemann.co.uk/hotlinks to complete a task or download information, please insert the code **5171P** at the website.

1 Rivers

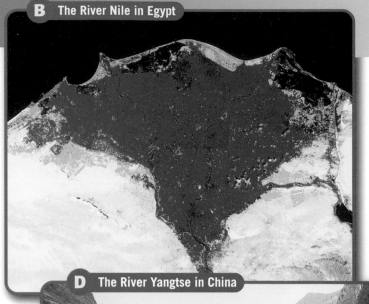

A The Niagara Falls in North America

B The River Nile in Egypt

D The River Yangtse in China

C The Kariba dam in Zimbabwe

E The River Amazon in Brazil

 ## Learn about

Rivers are important to people because they provide water, are used for transport and can be used to provide power. Rivers are constantly changing the shape of the landscape. From the *source* of the river to its *mouth*, the features of a river and its valley change significantly. In this unit you will learn about:

- locating a river section you are going to study
- what you need to find out when you study rivers
- what information you can collect in the field
- what the collected data means
- what conclusions you can draw.

F The River Tees in northern England

G A wedding party is escorted across flooded roads in North Yorkshire, 2000

H The Ganges is a sacred river for Hindus

I Transport on the River Nile

J Lower Falls, Colorado River, USA

Getting Technical ▼

- **Erosion** – wearing away the land and transporting the worn material away. This may be **vertical** or **horizontal** erosion in a river valley.

- **Deposition** – laying down eroded material

- **Weathering** – breaking down rock by exposure to weather conditions such as extreme heating or cooling, rainwater containing acid or biological activity. The rock is not transported away.

- **Source** – the beginning of a river

- **Waterfall** – a sharp break in the gradient of a river valley where water falls vertically

- **Gorge** – a steep-sided, almost vertical, valley cut by a river

- **Meanders** – a series of large sweeping bends in a river

- **Delta** – where a river splits into several parts before it meets the sea

- **Estuary** – where a river widens out in a funnel shape before it reaches the sea

Activities

1. Look carefully at the photographs on these two pages. Pick out the photographs where people are making use of rivers. Give a brief description of what the river is being used for in each photograph. 📖

2. **a** Select the photographs which show examples of the following river landscape features:

   i meanders **ii** waterfall **iii** gorge
   iv delta **v** estuary.

   b In a group, select any three of the landscape features you have identified. Discuss how you think they may have been formed. Write down your ideas, using diagrams and the words in the Getting Technical box to help you. 📖

What do you already know about river patterns and processes?

Some of the main patterns and processes found in a river that has its source in a highland area are shown in **A**. Sometimes a river has its source in a lowland area.

Upper course

A river's source is often in highland areas where there is usually more rainfall and surface run-off water.

Upland valley

V-shaped valley, the Lake District

Rocks and soil from the banks and valley sides may be broken down by weathering.

Middle section

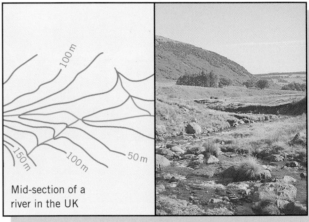

Mid-section of a river in the UK

Height (metres above sea level)

The river runs downstream from its source, cutting down its valley by **vertical erosion**. Valley sides are steep and there are usually large rocks on the river bed. Waterfalls are often found in this section.

The **gradient** of the river is gentler here and the channel is wider. Tributaries, surface run-off and ground water have increased the volume of the river. There is less vertical erosion and more lateral erosion.

Length of river from source to mouth

Gradient or slope decreases

Average speed of the river increases

Size of the river increases

Size of the rocks on the bed of the river decreases

More vertical erosion ➤ More lateral erosion

Waterfall in Swinner Gill, Swaledale

Activities

① Study the information about the long profile of a river in **A**. Imagine that you were following the river from its source to its mouth (from left to right in **A**). Write a description of the main changes that you would expect to see in the river and its valley. You could use the writing frame below to help start you off. 📖

The start of a river or its _____ is usually in _____ because _____ . The main features of the river valley at this point include _____ . As the river flows downstream, the gradient becomes _____ . The next section is called the _____ of the river. At this point the river changes and becomes _____ .

Lower course or flood plain

Meandering River
Dee, Clwyd

The river is usually wider and deeper here. There is more lateral erosion where the river cuts wide sweeping bends or meanders.

② Look at the annotated sketch **B** of the photograph of the upper course of the river. Draw a similar sketch of the photographs showing the middle section and lower course. Label or annotate the sketches to show the main features you would expect to find in each section of the river.

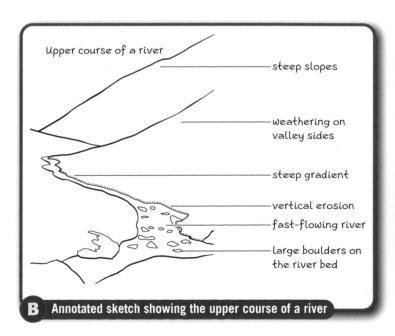

Upper course of a river
- steep slopes
- weathering on valley sides
- steep gradient
- vertical erosion
- fast-flowing river
- large boulders on the river bed

B   Annotated sketch showing the upper course of a river

Getting Technical ▾

Rivers wear away or **erode** the land they flow over. This is called **fluvial erosion**. A river may erode its channel vertically (downwards) or **laterally** (sideways).

Where is the river section you are going to study?

Using contour lines to identify features in a river valley

You can use an Ordnance Survey (OS) map to identify detailed features in a river valley. The pattern of the contour lines shows the changes in the shape and gradient of the river valley and the surrounding area.

Map **A** is an OS map showing parts of the valleys of the rivers Wharfe and Skirfare in Yorkshire. Look carefully at the contour patterns and other landscape features around the main rivers.

Contour lines form a 'V' pattern around the smaller tributary rivers. This indicates a steep gradient and steep valley sides, so the valley has a V-shaped profile.

River Wharfe – river meandering in the wide, flat valley floor.

Contour lines are close together, showing a steep slope on the valley sides.

Some smaller rivers and streams cut straight across the contour lines. This shows a very steep fall, usually a waterfall.

Contour lines are widely spaced, showing the river Skirfare has a gentle slope.

Road follows the flat section at the foot of the steep valley side.

River Skirfare

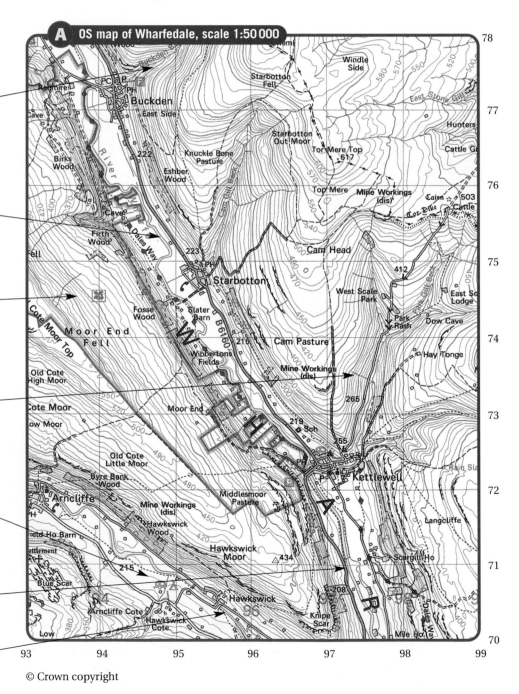

A OS map of Wharfedale, scale 1:50 000

© Crown copyright

Drawing cross-sections from contour lines

Diagram **B** shows how the contour patterns drawn on an OS map help you to identify what the landscape actually looks like. Cross-sections taken across the contour lines show a two-dimensional model of the landscape.

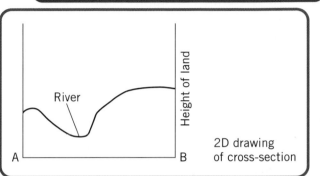

B Contour pattern and cross-section of a steep V-shaped river valley. The cross-section is taken from grid references 950760 to 970760 (A to B)

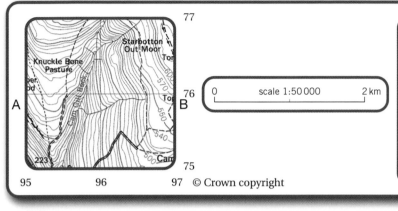

© Crown copyright

How to ...

... draw a cross-section

When you draw a cross-section, you are imagining that the land has been cut through to sea level and drawing a two-dimensional image or side profile of what the land looks like. Work through these four steps.

1   Place a strip of paper across the contour lines on the map where you want to take your section.

2   Mark the points where the contour lines cross the paper and write the height of each contour beside it.

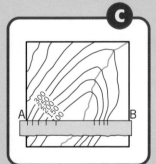

3   Take the paper off the map and use graph paper to construct the cross-section. The length of the cross-section forms the length of the bottom axis. Put sea level (0 metres) at the bottom of the side axis, then draw a scale that can fit in the heights you have marked on your cross-section.

4   You may want to label the cross-section with the landscape features identified on the map.

Activities

1 **a** Draw a scaled cross-section of part of a river valley from a suitable place on OS map **A**.

    b Label your cross-section using the following terms:

       river   flat/steep valley sides

    c Add a heading and a scale to your cross-section.

2 **Extension**

    Choose a place on map **A** with a different shape of valley and draw a cross-section to represent it. Label your drawing and add a heading.

Investigating rivers: what do you need to find out?

You have discovered in this unit that:

⊙ rivers are constantly changing the landscape by a process called fluvial erosion

⊙ different landscape features and processes are found at different places in a river's valley.

A fieldwork investigation on a stretch of river would give you the chance to test what you already know and to find out more about rivers.

Step 1: Asking questions

The first step in a geography fieldwork investigation is to ask questions.
What do you want to find out about rivers? Your title for this investigation could be:

How do landscapes and processes change in a river valley?

Here are some of the questions you could use to investigate the changes.

Do river valleys become wider further downstream?

Does the volume of water in a river increase further downstream?

Does the size of material in the river bed change as a river moves downstream?

On which side of a meander bend does the river flow fastest?

Is there any evidence of erosion and deposition on a meander section?

Is the height of the bank above the river greater in some sections than in others?

Is the deepest part of the river in the middle?

Measuring a stream for geography fieldwork

Does the river flow faster in the upper valley section or in the lower section?

Is the gradient of a river valley steeper in its upper course or in its lower course?

Activity

① In a group, study the enquiry questions above and decide which you are going to investigate. Then discuss what data you need and how you are going to collect it.

help!

It is better to work in a group because it makes data collection easier and safer. You must be sure to listen to advice about safety before you collect data in the field.

What information can you collect in the field?

Step 2: Collecting information

First, decide which questions you are going to investigate. You may add a few more, but they must be relevant to your study. Now decide how you are going to collect the information. It is important to measure and record your data accurately.

⑥ Most of the data you collect during a river investigation will be *primary data*, that is, data you actually go out and collect through measuring, sketching and observing.

⑥ You could collect *secondary data* about the river you are investigating by contacting the Environment Agency. Their website address is http://www.environment–agency.gov.uk. You could then compare this secondary data with your own data.

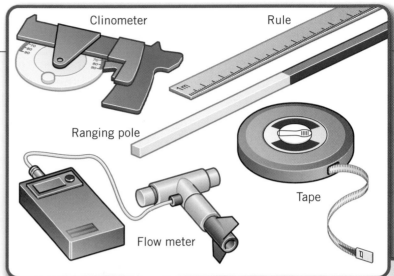

How to ...

... record data

Before you go on your field trip, you need to construct data collection sheets to record your data accurately. Here is an example of a data collection sheet used to investigate channel depth across a stretch of river. The group decided to record the depth of the river at three or more different sites in the river valley by taking six depth readings at regular intervals across the river.

Position	Depth of river					
	Readings (cm) (starting on left bank)					
	1	2	3	4	5	6
Site 1	3.5	8	8.5	10	4	2.5
Site 2						

A Useful equipment for a river investigation

Activity

① In your group, decide what information you need to collect for each of the questions you are going to investigate. Construct data collection sheets for each investigation. (ICT) (123)

What does your data mean?

Step 3: Showing your results

Once you have collected your data, you can start to write up your investigation and show what the data means. You will have collected a lot of measurements at different points along the river. You can use some of these to draw cross-sections of the river channel. You can also work out the speed of flow and the changes in volume, processes and landforms as you move to different sections of the river. Use a variety of maps, labelled sketches, photographs, cross-sections, graphs and written work to show this information. Look at the next four pages to discover new techniques for analysing and presenting your data.

Drawing a field sketch

When you were out collecting your data you may have sketched the river valley at different locations. You can now draw neater versions of your field sketches and annotate them to highlight the main features and processes. You can see a sketch and sketch plan that a student drew as part of her investigation in **A** and **B**. If you have taken images with a digital camera, you could load them onto a PC, annotate them and print them off to add to your investigation.

A Annotated sketch of the upper course of the study river

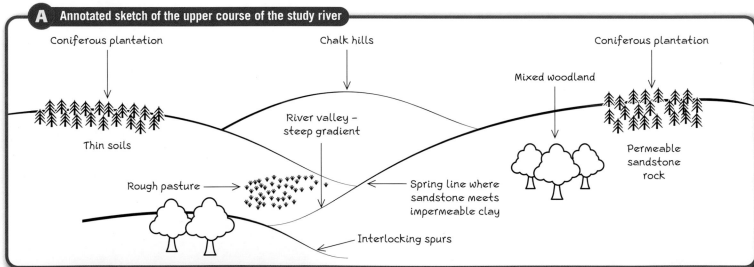

B Sketch plan of the mid-course of the study river

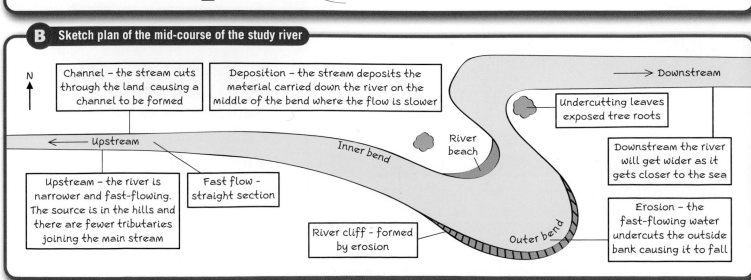

Drawing cross-sections

To draw the cross-section of a river, you need measurements of:

⊚ the depth of the river ⊚ the width of the river from bank to bank

⊚ the width of the channel ⊚ the height of the bank above the river.

How to ...

... draw a cross-section of a river

1 Look at the measurements you have collected and decide on a scale that will fit on your paper.

2 Start your section by drawing the width of the river. Make sure that you have enough room to draw in the river channel below it.

3 Look at the measurements for the height of the bank above the river level on both sides and mark in the position of both banks.

4 Measure the width of the channel bank to bank. Now draw in the banks.

5 Next you can mark in the river bed by using the measurements of the depth of the river from the surface and marking the points on the cross-section. Join the points together to show the river bed.

6 Add a scale and a heading.

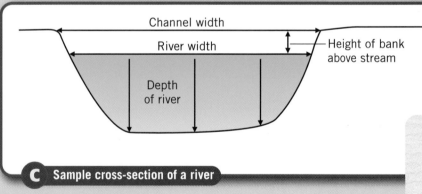

C Sample cross-section of a river

Getting Technical ▾

⊚ The amount of water flowing down a stream is known as the **discharge**. The discharge can be calculated by using this formula:

discharge = velocity × area

⊚ To work out the area of a cross-section of a river:

1 Calculate the average depth by adding all the depth readings and divide by the number of readings. In **D** the average would be (12 + 31 + 35 + 10)/4 = 22 cm.

2 Multiply the average depth by the average width of the river to give the area. In **D** the area would be 22 × 120 = 2640 cm².

Width of channel from bank to bank: 155 cm

Width of river: 120 cm

Height of bank above the river:
   left side: 25 cm
   right side: 53 cm

Depth of river:

	Left bank			Right bank
Reading	1	2	3	4
Depth (cm)	12	31	35	10

D Readings at a cross-section of a river

Activity

① The figures in **D** are taken from a different section of the river shown in **C** below. Draw a cross-section by following the steps carefully. **123**

Drawing long profiles and graphs

You can show many of the changes you recorded in your fieldwork by drawing a long profile of the river you have been studying. This long profile will help you to make a summary of your investigation. Follow the steps in the How to ... box to draw your own long profile.

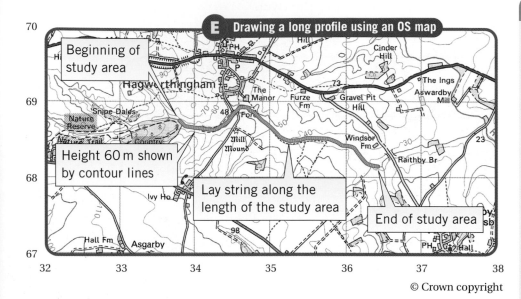

E   Drawing a long profile using an OS map

© Crown copyright

Activity

2 Using a suitable OS map, find a section of a river where you can see clear differences in height and changes in its features. You could use map **A** on page 8. Draw a long profile of the section using the instructions in the How to ... box. Mark on your profile any changes you can see on the map. Look for evidence of the contour patterns showing valley width or steepness, or features such as waterfalls and bridges. ①②③

How to ...

... draw a long profile

You will need an OS map of the section of river you were investigating.

1   Use a piece of string to measure the length of the section of river you were investigating on the map. This will be the length of the long profile for the horizontal axis.

2   Estimate the height of the river where your study started by looking for evidence of spot heights or contour lines on the map. Now look for the height of the point where your study finished. The difference between these two heights will give you the height of your profile for the vertical axis.

3   Now place a straight edge of paper along the length of the river and carefully mark each point where the river crosses a contour line. Write the height of the contour line beside your mark. Put your paper along the bottom of the profile. Mark off changes in height. Join up the points to draw your profile.

4   Label the profile with the information you have collected at your three study sites, including the measurements and main features. You could use photos, sketches or cross-sections.

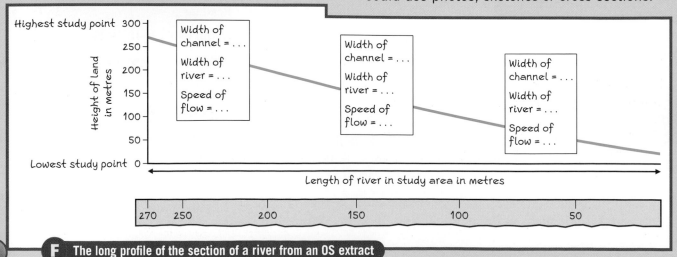

F   The long profile of the section of a river from an OS extract

Graphs and proportional lines

Some of the data you have collected may be difficult to show well in a profile or a sketch. It may be better to show it by drawing graphs or proportional lines. Examples of such data include:

- ⑥ the speed of flow, or **velocity**, in different sections of the river
- ⑥ the size and shape of bed material found in different sections
- ⑥ changes in velocity across the river (see **G** below).

Look at **G** to see how a set of data can be shown in two different ways.

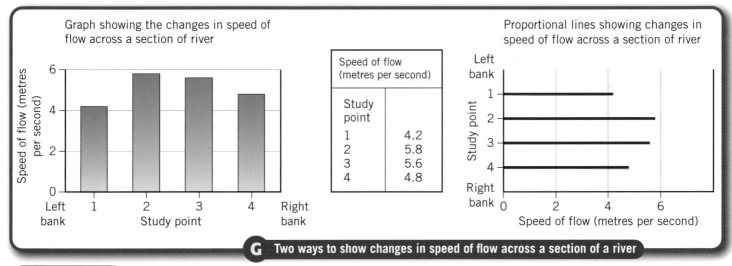

G **Two ways to show changes in speed of flow across a section of a river**

Activities

③ Some students from the Deepings School measured the velocity of the Winceby Beck at five points down its length. They took three readings at each point. Copy out their results in the table below, and work out the average speed of flow at each of the five river study points. (123)

Study points along the river's course:						
Nearest the source	**1**	**2**	**3**	**4**	**5**	**Nearest the mouth**
Velocity (m/sec)						
Reading 1	4.2	3.4	3.1	5.2	6.3	**Reading 1**
Reading 2	4.8	4.0	2.9	5.0	5.5	**Reading 2**
Reading 3	4.0	3.8	3.5	4.1	6.1	**Reading 3**
Average						

④ Now draw a graph or proportional lines to show how the speed of flow changes along the course of the river. You might like to use a spreadsheet package to draw the graph. (123) (ICT)

⑤ Look at the graph or lines you have drawn for question **4** and write a comment about what is shown. You may use the following writing frame to start you off. 📖

> **Comment on the changes in speed of flow along a river's profile**
>
> The fastest flowing section of the river is at study point _____ , recording an average speed of _____ metres/sec. The slowest section is at study point _____ which records an average speed of _____ metres/sec.
>
> This shows that ...
>
> The reason for this pattern/result may be ...

Step 4: Drawing conclusions

Once you have collected enough data and displayed the results using a range of techniques, you must now draw some conclusions about your investigation and evaluate your work. The more data you collect, the more reliable your conclusions will be.

help!

A conclusion:

- looks at all the work you have done
- links the results to the questions you asked in the beginning.

An evaluation:

- looks at the strengths and the weaknesses of the work as a whole
- makes suggestions about further investigations you might carry out.

Conclusion

The main enquiry question was:

How do landscapes and processes change in a river valley?

The first part of your conclusion should give a general statement about what you found from your investigations. You could start your conclusion by writing:

> From my study of the different sections of the river ... I found that the river landscapes and processes did change as it moved downstream. The main changes were ...

Now give details including figures and refer to the diagrams, maps and graphs you have drawn.

Evaluation

Your evaluation should finish off your enquiry. It refers to the whole piece of work and you should make a note of the strengths and weaknesses of the project. You should mention what went well and what didn't go so well. Go on to suggest how it could be improved next time. You also need to suggest ideas for further investigation of the same topic.

You could start your evaluation by writing:

> I learned a lot about river landscapes and processes from doing this enquiry. I also learned how important it was to ...

You could then go on to say:

> We had some difficulty collecting the information because ...

and finally give suggestions of how you could extend your investigations:

> It would be good to go and do some further study on ...

Activity

6 Now that you have learned to collect primary data, used different methods of presenting your data, drawn conclusions and evaluated your work, you can write an investigation using secondary data. You could, for example, use data from the Environment Agency's website. Go to www.heinemann.co.uk/hotlinks and insert code 5171P. You should try to get information for a complete stretch of river rather than just the two or three sections that you studied in your fieldwork. (ICT) (📖) (123)

Review and reflect

Activities

1 a In this unit you have learned about river valley processes, landscape patterns and how to complete a fieldwork investigation. Complete a spider diagram like the one below to make a summary of the facts you have learned while studying this section. Add any further relevant facts, including details from your fieldwork.

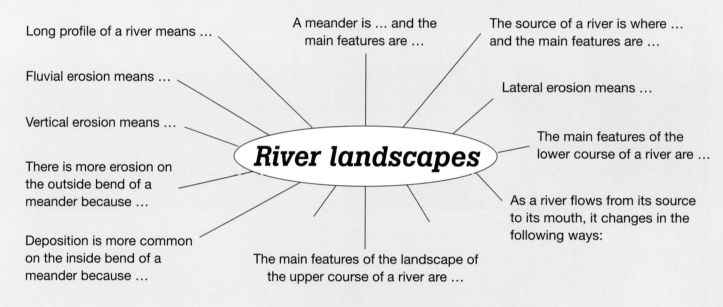

Long profile of a river means …

Fluvial erosion means …

Vertical erosion means …

There is more erosion on the outside bend of a meander because …

Deposition is more common on the inside bend of a meander because …

A meander is … and the main features are …

The main features of the landscape of the upper course of a river are …

River landscapes

The source of a river is where … and the main features are …

Lateral erosion means …

The main features of the lower course of a river are …

As a river flows from its source to its mouth, it changes in the following ways:

b Use the terms in your spider diagram to start a geography word bank.

2 Now you have learned to carry out a fieldwork enquiry on a river landscape you will be able to apply the same skills to any other enquiry by using these steps:

⊚ **Deciding on a title** – this is often in the form of a question, which may start with the words:

What is …? Where are …? How …? Who …? Why …?

It may also state a **hypothesis** (a theory) which you set out to prove or disprove through your investigation.

⊚ **Collecting information** – you must decide what information you need and where you can get it, and design data collection sheets. Look back at page 11 to remind you.

⊚ **Showing results** – you can use many different methods to show your results: maps, graphs, sketches, photographs, written work. You can see examples on pages 12–15.

⊚ **Drawing conclusions and evaluating** – you must reflect back to the original title of your study and attempt to answer it using evidence from the data you have collected. Look back at page 16.

Position	Depth of river					
	Readings (cm) (starting on left bank)					
	1	2	3	4	5	6
Site 1	3.5	8	8.5	10	4	2.5
Site 2						

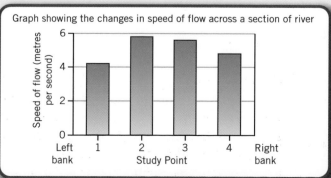

Graph showing the changes in speed of flow across a section of river

Learn about

The Earth's scenery or landscape varies from place to place and is changing all the time. Knowing and understanding about the processes that cause these changes can help people manage the problems they can create. In this unit you will learn:

🌀 how weathering and erosion affect coastlines

🌀 how the coast is shaped by the sea in different ways

🌀 what causes some parts of the coast to collapse

🌀 how people try to manage the coast by protecting it against the sea.

Activity

1. Write down five geographical questions you could ask someone about the scene in photograph **A**. Think of questions that would help you to find out how this farm on top of a cliff has been destroyed. Use words like *why*, *where*, *what* and *how* in your questions.

How is our coastline formed?

The UK's coastline stretches for over 10 000 kilometres around the country. It attracts millions of people, both for its wild and natural beauty and its sandy beaches and exciting nightlife. Coasts change rapidly – they are dynamic places – and the natural processes of **weathering** and **erosion** are acting on the rocks along the coast all the time to shape it into the bays, beaches and **headlands** that people like to visit. How does this happen?

What is weathering?

The landscapes of the world are constantly changing. Rain, sun, wind and frost are breaking down even the hardest rocks into smaller pieces before they are carried away. This process is known as weathering. There are three main types of weathering.

Mechanical weathering is caused by changes in temperature. In freeze–thaw weathering, water gets into cracks in a rock and freezes. As it freezes it expands. Repeated freezing and melting eventually cause the rock to split.

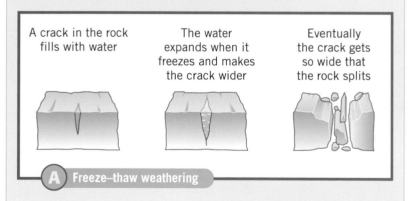

A crack in the rock fills with water

The water expands when it freezes and makes the crack wider

Eventually the crack gets so wide that the rock splits

A Freeze–thaw weathering

Biological weathering is caused by the action of plants on rocks. Plants can grow in cracks in rocks. As their roots develop they can force the cracks to widen and the rocks to fall apart. Lichens and mosses can also grow on rocks. They make the rock surface slowly crumble.

C Biological weathering in Majorca

Chemical weathering is caused by the action of water on the chemicals in rock. Rainwater is made slightly acidic as it falls through the atmosphere. When it comes into contact with rock, it dissolves some of it away. Chemical weathering is most effective in warm, wet areas. You can find more information on how chemical weathering affects limestone on page 93. Sea water can also cause chemical weathering.

B The cracks in this limestone pavement are caused by chemical weathering

Activities

1. Write a sentence to describe what *weathering* means.

2. Draw a set of diagrams like those in **A** to describe how biological weathering occurs.

3. Put these sentences in order to describe how chemical weathering occurs.

   ◎ The weakly acidic rainwater attacks the rock.

   ◎ Rainwater becomes acid as it falls through the atmosphere.

   ◎ The rock dissolves and crumbles away.

4. Carry out a survey of your own school to find out where the building is being weathered. Think of some enquiry questions you could ask about where the weathering is found, e.g. how high up or on which side of the building it is.

What is erosion?

Getting Technical ▾

Weathering is a process that weakens and breaks up rocks. The wearing away of the rocks and the removal of the weathered material is called **erosion**. The loose weathered material can be carried away by rivers, wind, the sea, ice – or by people. The work of these **agents of erosion** is explained below.

Rivers are constantly wearing away tiny pieces of rock from their banks and their beds. These particles are carried away by the river. When a river is in flood it can carry huge boulders.

A River erosion on the River Clwyd

B The Mittens in Arizona, USA

If you walk along a beach when there is a strong **wind**, you will feel the sand blowing against your face. The particles carried by the wind blast away the rocks in their path, sometimes forming weird and wonderful shapes like this.

C Waves erode the cliffs on the Oregon coast

Waves constantly batter our shores and wear away the cliffs. Eroded particles are carried away by the waves or by currents and are deposited on beaches. Material can also be moved along beaches by waves.

D These rocks in Greenland have been eroded by the movement of ice

In mountain and polar regions, huge masses of **ice** move down valleys and across plains. As they travel, they pick up rocks and stones which grind away at the ground surface below, wearing down the land like sandpaper. The material they move collects in huge mounds at the end of the valley.

E This footpath in the Yorkshire Dales has been eroded by millions of feet

People cause erosion in many different ways. Bulldozers can be used to dig out large amounts of soil. People can wear away a surface just by walking over it. They can also remove trees and other plants which hold the soil together, allowing water and wind to remove the soil more easily.

Washing the dishes is like erosion. The force of the water and the scrubbing you do remove the dirt from the plates. Throwing the water away **transports** the waste material down the drain to another place, where it is **deposited**. On a larger scale, mountains, valleys and coasts are shaped and changed by water, wind and ice. Erosion wears away the land; the loose material is transported to another place where it may be deposited to make new landforms.

I'm just eroding the dishes!

Activities

① **a** Write two or three sentences to explain the difference between weathering and erosion. Use words like *breaking down*, *transportation* and *wearing away*.

b Add the words *erosion* and *weathering* to your word bank.

② **Odd one out**

1	Freeze–thaw	**5**	Transport	**9**	River
2	Weathering	**6**	Mechanical	**10**	People
3	Biological	**7**	Deposit	**11**	Tree roots
4	Wind	**8**	Erosion	**12**	Glacier

For each set below, decide which is the odd one out, and give a reason for your choice.

Set A	1	2	9	**Set D**	11	7	3
Set B	2	7	6	**Set E**	4	5	11
Set C	5	9	12	**Set F**	7	8	10

③ **Extension**

Which of the following groups of people would find weathering a positive thing? Which would find it a negative thing? Explain your answers.

House-owners   **Farmers**   **Architects**

④ Make your own scale of hardness using things you can find at home. Test five materials by trying to scratch them with a nail file or emery board. You could include glass, steel, concrete or wax. Complete a table of your results.

Scale of hardness	Material
Hardest 1	
2	
3	
4	
Softest 5	

Hard and soft rocks

The rate at which rocks are weathered and eroded has a lot to do with how hard they are. Some rocks are soft – they crumble easily in your hands or they are washed away very easily, for example **clay** or **chalk**. Other rocks are made of particles or crystals which are very hard or which are cemented together to make them very resistant to erosion. Rocks like this include **granite** and **marble**.

How do waves shape our coast?

Waves are responsible for most of the landforms we see on our coasts. They are eroding the land and moving material all day and all night. But most erosion happens on stormy days when strong winds drive large waves against the shore. These waves have such force that they can break off bits of rocks from cliffs and move vast amounts of sand and shingle from one place to another. The sea erodes the land, transports the eroded material and deposits it elsewhere. A series of coastal landforms are created, some of them by erosion, some by deposition.

A Runswick Bay, North Yorkshire

D Aerial view of Chesil Beach, Dorset

E Mount Cliff, Beaumaris

B Vertical cliffs of the Seven Sisters, East Sussex

C Country Park, East Lothian showing saltmarsh, sandflats and spits

Activities

1. With a partner, look at photographs **A–E**. Put them into pairs and look for connections between them. For example, **A** and **B** both show cliffs. There is more than one correct answer – your answer is right as long as you have found a good connection.

2. Copy the table below. Write down the letters for each of your pairs with a short explanation of the connection.

Pair	Connection
A and B	Both show cliffs

How does the sea erode the coast?

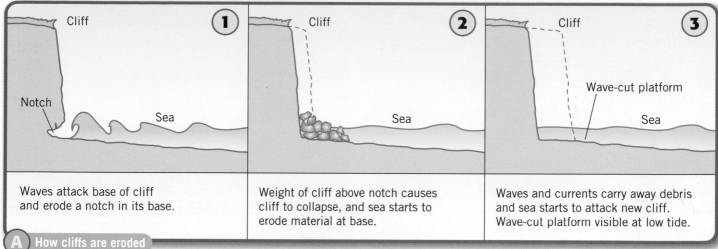

Cliff ①	Cliff ②	Cliff ③
Notch Sea	Sea	Wave-cut platform Sea
Waves attack base of cliff and erode a notch in its base.	Weight of cliff above notch causes cliff to collapse, and sea starts to erode material at base.	Waves and currents carry away debris and sea starts to attack new cliff. Wave-cut platform visible at low tide.

A How cliffs are eroded

Erosion occurs in different ways along the coast when powerful waves crash against the foot of a cliff.

- The waves hurl sand and shingle against the cliff. This scrapes at the rocks on the cliff, rather like sandpaper.

- Waves also trap air in the cracks in the rock, and the pressure created causes large pieces of rock to break off.

Softer rocks are eroded more easily and wear away more quickly forming bays. Harder rocks form cliffs and stand out as headlands. Photograph **B** shows what happens when bands of hard and soft rock reach the coast.

How to ...

... describe a photograph of a coastline

1 Begin with a general statement, e.g. *The picture shows a coast with bays and headlands.*

2 Go on to give greater detail about the type of rock you can see, the colours and the shapes that they make. Use words like *vertical*, *angular*, *rounded*.

3 Mention whether the rock is bare or covered in vegetation. Is there any sign of people or their activities?

4 Try to find something in the picture to give you a scale and try to give sizes to what you are describing.

B This coastline in Pembrokeshire is formed of hard and soft bands of rock

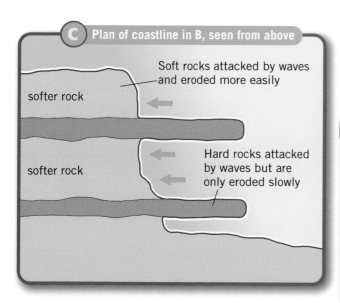

C Plan of coastline in B, seen from above

Soft rocks attacked by waves and eroded more easily

softer rock

softer rock

Hard rocks attacked by waves but are only eroded slowly

Activities

1 Create a word list that would help you describe the coast in photograph **B**.

2 Use your word list and the How to ... box to help you write a description of the coast in the photograph.

3 Use diagram **C** to help you explain how the headlands and bays in **B** were formed. You may need to draw another diagram to help you.

Features of coastal erosion

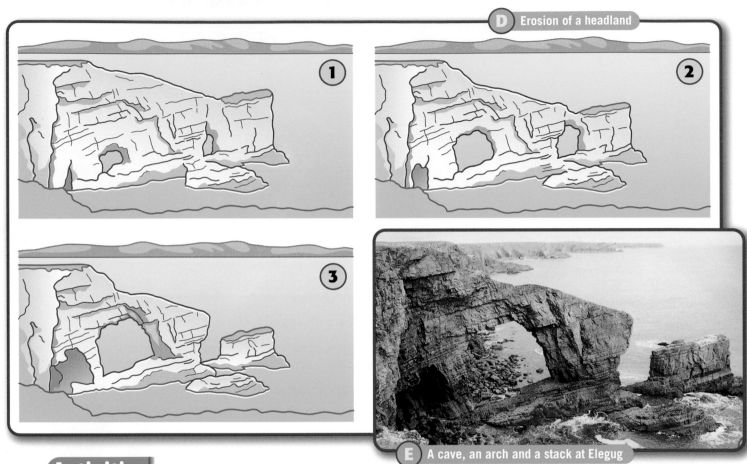

D Erosion of a headland

① ② ③

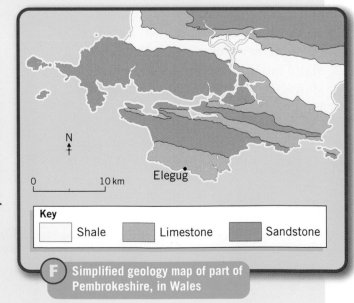

E A cave, an arch and a stack at Elegug

Activities

④ The three diagrams in **D** show how the sea erodes cliffs to develop other landforms (see **E**). Make a sketch of the photo and then use the labels below to annotate your diagrams.

⦿ The sea attacks small cracks and opens them.

⦿ The cracks get larger and develop into a small **cave**.

⦿ When the cave wears right through the headland, an **arch** forms.

⦿ More erosion causes the arch to collapse. This leaves a pillar of rock called a **stack** in the sea.

⑤ Map **F** shows that the area is made up of several different types of rocks, which are shown in the key.

  a Trace or draw a sketch map of the coast.

  b Label the bays and headlands.

  c Shade the rock types.

⑥ **a** Which type of rock forms the headlands?

  b Which type of rock forms the bays? Why?

⑦ Think of two reasons why a coast shaped like this is useful to people.

⑧ Add the words *cliff*, *headland*, *bay* and *wave-cut platform* to your word bank and explain what they mean. 📖

N
↑

0   10 km   Elegug

Key

☐ Shale   ▨ Limestone   ▨ Sandstone

F Simplified geology map of part of Pembrokeshire, in Wales

Features of coastal deposition

Material that has been eroded by the sea is carried along the coast by a process known as **longshore drift** (see **G**).

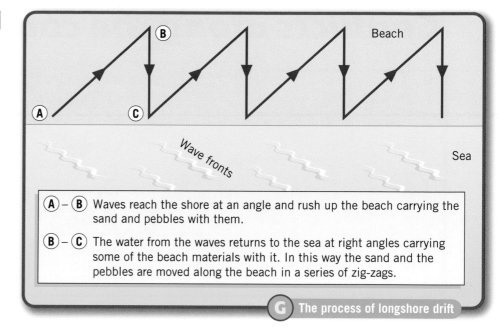

(A) – (B) Waves reach the shore at an angle and rush up the beach carrying the sand and pebbles with them.

(B) – (C) The water from the waves returns to the sea at right angles carrying some of the beach materials with it. In this way the sand and the pebbles are moved along the beach in a series of zig-zags.

G The process of longshore drift

Eventually, the material carried along the coast by longshore drift has to be dumped somewhere. This is called **deposition**. Deposition often takes place where a river mouth or bay cuts into the coastline and interrupts the longshore drift. Over many years the deposited material is added to and grows out across the river mouth or bay to form a long finger of sand or shingle known as a **spit**. You can see a photograph of a spit in **C** on page 22.

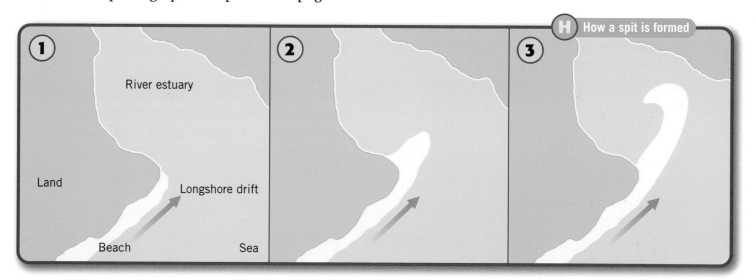

H How a spit is formed

Activity

9 Copy the set of diagrams in **H** which show how a spit develops. Annotate them in the same way as the sketches you drew for the cave, arch and stack. Use the words *longshore drift*, *deposition* and *beach* in your annotations. You could scan your drawings and annotate them using a computer. **ICT**

Conflicts along the coast

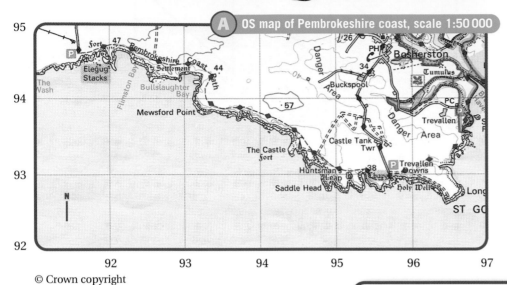

A OS map of Pembrokeshire coast, scale 1:50 000

© Crown copyright

Coastal areas are popular for the development of tourism, industry and settlement. But these land uses do not always exist together without affecting one another. There are some which **conflict** with each other. On the area shown on **A** the army shooting range (Danger Area) conflicts with the wishes of tourists to walk along the coastal path.

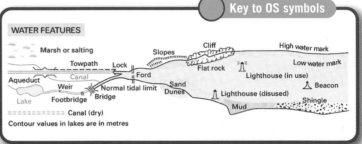

Key to OS symbols

WATER FEATURES

Marsh or salting
Towpath · Lock
Aqueduct
Weir
Lake · Footbridge · Bridge · Normal tidal limit
Canal (dry)
Contour values in lakes are in metres

Slopes · Cliff · High water mark
Low water mark
Ford · Flat rock · Lighthouse (in use)
Sand · Beacon
Dunes · Lighthouse (disused)
Shingle
Mud

Activities

① OS map **A** shows an area of the coast in Pembrokeshire.

a Imagine you are taking a walk along the coastal path. Draw an annotated sketch map of the route you would take, labelling at least four features of erosion and deposition that you have learned about in this unit so far. You could choose from *stack, beach, cliff, wave-cut platform, headland, bay* and *arch*. Elegug Stacks is shown on photograph **E**, page 24.

b Write a description of your route, using six-figure grid references to locate the features. Don't forget to use compass directions to help you describe where you are going.

c Describe what three of the features look like.

② Look for all the different types of land use along the coast that are shown in the map. Then construct a **conflict matrix** to show which land uses conflict with one another. Explain why two of these conflicts occur.

How to...

... construct a conflict matrix

Copy the table opposite. Choose six different groups who use the coast and write them in the green user group boxes. Complete the unshaded boxes in the matrix by considering where there is conflict between two users.

◎ If there is a conflict, put a cross.

◎ If groups can exist without interfering with one another, put a tick.

◎ If neither, put zero.

1	2	3	4	5	6
1					
	2				
		3			
			4		
				5	
					6

USER GROUPS

Why do cliffs collapse?

B B C HOMEPAGE | WORLD SERVICE | EDUCATION

B B C NEWS *UPDATED EVERY MINUTE OF EVERY DAY*

Front Page	12 January, 1999, 08.00 GMT
World	**Beachy Head collapse**
UK	More news soon...

UK Politics
Business
Sci/Tech
Health
Education
Entertainment
Talking Point
In Depth
Audio Video

B B C SPORT>>

Search BBC News Online

[ ] GO

Beachy Head collapse

A huge chunk of the famous cliff at Beachy Head near Eastbourne in Sussex crashed into the sea in a massive landslide over the weekend.

A 200-metre section of cliff loosened by persistent rain crashed onto the beach near the lighthouse.

The rockfall, which can be seen from 5 km out to sea, has been blamed on climate change by some people.

Ray Kent, a spokesman for the Environment Agency, said: 'This was a massive fall, hundreds of thousands of tonnes have fallen away from the cliff face. It has caused very significant damage to Beachy Head. It is basically down to climate change. The level of the sea is rising, so bigger waves are hitting against the cliff base, causing bigger vibrations to reverberate up the cliff.

'This was combined with twelve days of extremely wet weather during the Christmas period. The chalk was absolutely sodden so the combination has caused the rock to fall away. Unfortunately, it could be the shape of things to come.'

Freezing temperatures are believed to have expanded the water which seeped into the chalk, causing it to crumble and sheer off.

Coastguards have warned people to stay away from the edge of the cliff, a notorious suicide spot, as experts try to establish whether further rockfalls could be expected.

© **B B C** ∧∧ Back to top

Activities

❶ Study the Internet page reporting the cliff collapse at Beachy Head.

a Write out the points that suggest why the event occurred. Underline the reasons in three different colours to show whether it was the weather, the sea or the land which was thought to be to blame.

b Use your notes to help you write an explanation of why the cliff collapse occurred. Use an *explanation genre* writing frame to help you with your account. 📖

❷ Visit the BBC News website or the Environment Agency website at www.heinemann.co.uk/hotlinks (insert code 5171P) to find out about other cliff collapses that are occurring around the coast of the British Isles. (ICT)

Case Study
Save our homes!

The tiny settlement of Birling Gap near Beachy Head is teetering on the edge of the cliffs. The English Channel is creeping closer every year, as it has done for thousands of years, eating away at the soft chalk. If nothing is done, the houses will almost certainly slip into the sea in the near future. The residents want sea defences to be put in place to protect the cliff, but English Nature, the Government's wildlife adviser, is against the idea. So is the National Trust, who own three of the cottages. You can read what some people think about the future of Birling Gap in **B**.

A Birling Gap in 1900 and 1999

There are three houses still lived in and a lovely pub in our hamlet. We want a small wall, or **revetment**, to be built at the base of the cliff so that the waves will stop undercutting the cliff. The sea defence would NOT detract from the famous view of the Seven Sisters cliffs and the beach would be safer!
Birling Gap resident

Birling Gap is a Site of Special Scientific Interest because of the way the land and sea intersect at the shoreline, for its sections of exposed chalk which are very interesting geologically, and for the special habitats and shelters it provides for birdlife and animals. Any attempts to protect the Gap would cause problems further along the coast and probably wouldn't work anyway. They would also spoil the natural appearance of the beach.
Spokesperson for English Nature

The sea cannot be held back forever. The cottages will eventually fall into the sea because the sea will erode any protection that we put there. However, a small revetment will hold back the sea for the next 15–20 years and would be relatively cheap to build.
Civil engineer

We own the land and three of the cottages in this area. The National Trust tries to accept and work with natural coastal processes and we realise that we will have to lose land on the coast. We cannot support the building of the revetment and we have offered to buy the three occupied cottages from their private owners.
Spokesperson for National Trust

Activity

1 In groups of three or four, prepare a role play exercise. Each person plays the role of someone in **B** who is involved in the Birling Gap issue and prepares a speech for an Enquiry into the future of the hamlet.

B Some views on the future of Birling Gap

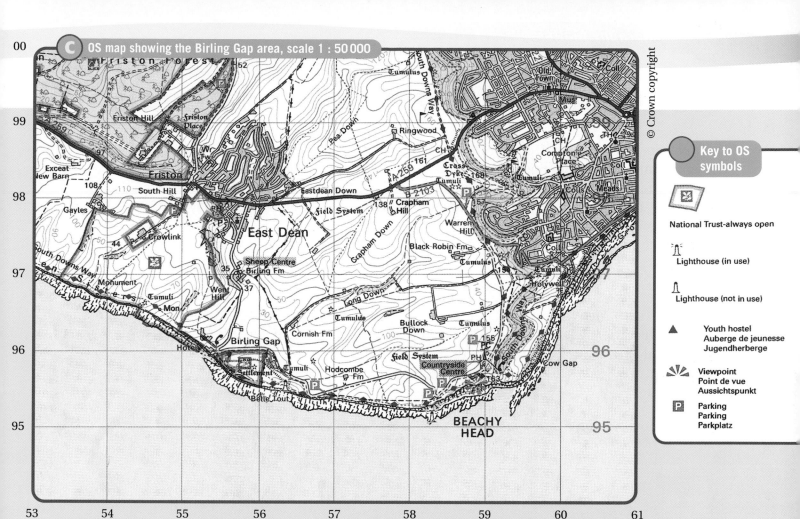

C OS map showing the Birling Gap area, scale 1 : 50 000

Key to OS symbols

National Trust-always open

Lighthouse (in use)

Lighthouse (not in use)

▲ Youth hostel
Auberge de jeunesse
Jugendherberge

Viewpoint
Point de vue
Aussichtspunkt

P Parking
Parking
Parkplatz

Activity

2 Imagine you are a reporter who is sent to cover the story about Birling Gap falling into the sea. You are going to visit several people to interview them for your Sunday supplement but your secretary has mislaid their addresses. All you have are the notes you made of their names and roughly where they can be found.

a Try to locate the homes of all the people on the table. Write down the six-figure grid reference for each one.

b Discuss how you decided on the chosen locations. What problems did you have, and why?

<u>Alice Richards</u> is just 10 and loves to go down to the beach in the bay when the tide is out. She and her mother take a picnic down from their house perched on top of the cliff.

<u>Bill and Anna Humphreys</u> are proprietors of the Birling Gap Hotel, a large faded Victorian building. Being close to the sea, it attracts visitors from busy cities.

<u>Paul Taylor</u> has spent many years building up his collection of rare breeds of sheep. He is about to buy some more land on Went Hill so that he can graze them more easily.

<u>Melanie Brown</u> lives in a farm not far from the cliffs. She has watched the road to Beachy Head get busier and busier: on a hot Sunday afternoon the car parks along the road to her farm are overflowing.

<u>Mark and Louise Roberts</u> live in the most unusual place on the map. They have just spent thousands and thousands of pounds moving their lighthouse back from the top of the cliffs.

<u>Karen Banks</u> is warden at the Youth Hostel. It is handy for the South Downs Way and only a short walk from the old town.

How can the coast be managed?

It is not only cliffs that have to be protected from the sea. Some lowland areas of the coast are constantly at risk from flooding. It is the job of the local council to protect its residents from the effects of coastal erosion and flooding. They must choose the best way to manage the coast by deciding how much to spend on protection against the sea and deciding what types of protection should be built.

Case Study: Protecting Towyn from the sea

In the winter of 1990 the little town of Towyn on the North Wales coast was flooded when the sea broke through the sea wall. When the flood was over the Council had to decide how to protect the town from future flooding events. They asked for a technical report, and decided to use four types of protection against flooding.

A Flooding in Towyn in 1990

N

Towyn • Rhyl
Colwyn Bay

0   20 km

B Towyn, North Wales

Technical report

The coastal lowlands at Towyn have been protected by embankments since the eighteenth century. Much of the land around Towyn is only just above sea level, and a sea wall was built to protect the land from the sea.

On 26 February 1990 a deep depression generated very strong winds blowing across North Wales from the Irish Sea. They reached 70–80 knots (140–160 km/hour) at their strongest. Waves were breaking at 2 m above their normal height. The sea broke through the protective wall at about 5 m above sea level and quickly flooded large areas of land.

Very little sediment was carried landward during the flood, because longshore drift had recently removed shingle and sand from in front of the sea wall and embankment.

Activities

Use map **C** and other information from these pages to answer the following questions.

① Lay a piece of tracing paper over the map. Shade in the area that would have been covered by the floods if the waves were 5 m above sea level when they broke through the old wall. Use the How to ... box to help you.

② Name four different types of land use that would have been affected by the flood. Give six-figure grid references for the land uses you mention.

③ a How long is the new sea wall?

   b How much would it have cost to build?

   c How much would it have cost to extend the new sea wall to the car park at 988797? 123

How to ...

... use contour lines to help you estimate

⊚ On your tracing, draw in the coastline.

⊚ Find the 5 m contour line and trace along that.

⊚ Shade in the area inside your lines and use the grid lines to estimate the area that the flood would have covered. Remember: each grid square is one kilometre square.

C OS map of Towyn, scale 1:25 000

new sea wall

Groynes
Baysville
Foryd Br
Yr Hafod
Foryd
Kinmel Bay/
Bae Cinmel
99
FB
FB
Holiday
Centres
A 548
Sch
Tir Prince
Raceway
Towyn
Ppg
Sta
Pol
Sta
PO
Caravan
Park
Henllys
Ty Mawr
Holiday Park
Plâs
Llwyd
Ppg
Sta
Sewage
Works
Gors
Tir Llwyd
Industrial Estate
Fachell
Belgrano
Morfa
Rhuddlan
KINMEL BAY AND TOWYN C
Pensarn
5 m
Gors
Cottage
Gors
Wood
Gors Road
River Gele / Afon Gele
5 m
Glan-y-gors
Sheepfold
Pont y
Morfa
Pen-y-bont
Sun
Farm
For
Porth
Farm
Weir
Schs
Col
ABERGELE C

Mean Low Water
North Wales Path
Pipe Lines
Outlet
Caravan Parks
Holiday
Centres
FB
FB
FB

95 96 97 98 99

© Crown copyright

D

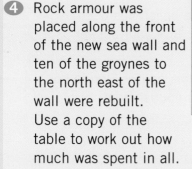

A sea wall costs £5000 per metre to build

Rock armour costs £1000 per metre

Beach nourishment is cheap – sand is added to the beach to make it higher

These groynes cost £10 000 each to build.

❹ Rock armour was placed along the front of the new sea wall and ten of the groynes to the north east of the wall were rebuilt. Use a copy of the table to work out how much was spent in all.

Type of defence	Cost
Sea wall	£
Groynes	£
Rock armour	£
Total	£

❺ Why do you think the Council was willing to spend this much money on rebuilding the wall?

❻ Beach nourishment was also used to protect the northern end of the new wall. Explain why this had to be replaced every year.

❼ Why might people living further along the coast to the east be concerned about the rebuilding of the groynes?

Case Study
Managing the beaches in Florida, USA

Large stretches of the east coast of Florida have been eroded away over the past century. These losses occurred where beaches were starved of sand because sea defences were built further along the coast to protect the hotels and condominiums (blocks of flats).

Beaches protect coasts because they stop waves reaching the land and eroding it. This part of the Florida coast also suffers from hurricanes. These produce huge destructive waves that remove tonnes and tonnes of sand from the beaches.

Florida spends over US $8.5 million each year on erosion management of its coasts. This is because it relies heavily on the income it receives from the millions of visitors who come to enjoy its white sandy beaches. At Miami Beach every dollar invested each year in beach nourishment returns 700 dollars in income from tourists.

Some conservationists think that protecting the beach with 'hard' engineering (such as groynes and sea walls) is wrong and that the coast should be allowed to erode naturally. This will supply material which will build up the coast in another place. This method of management is called 'managed retreat' and is shown in **C**.

A Sarasota beach in Florida

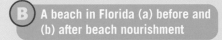

B A beach in Florida (a) before and (b) after beach nourishment

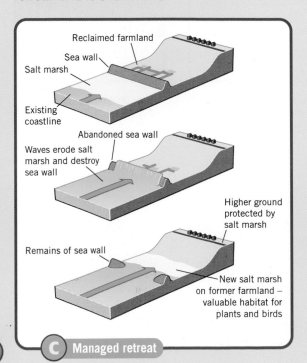

C Managed retreat

Reclaimed farmland
Sea wall
Salt marsh
Existing coastline

Abandoned sea wall
Waves erode salt marsh and destroy sea wall

Higher ground protected by salt marsh
Remains of sea wall
New salt marsh on former farmland – valuable habitat for plants and birds

Activities

1. Estimate how much extra beach has been created in photograph **B**. Give your answer as a percentage.

2. Give three reasons why this part of Florida has been protected by beach nourishment.

3. Do you think that managed retreat is a good way to manage the coast? Give reasons for your answer.

Review and reflect

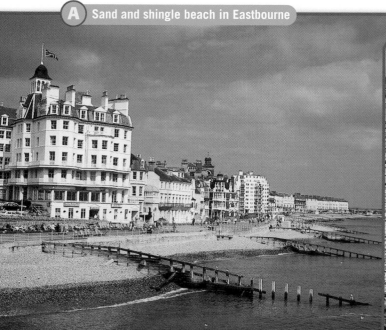

A Sand and shingle beach in Eastbourne

B Chalk cliffs at Selwicks Bay, Humberside

Activities

1. Look at the two photographs. For which photograph is each of these statements likely to be true? Try to give a reason for your answer. If you think that the statement is true for both photographs, give a reason for each of them.

   a Chemical weathering is occurring.

   b Material is being moved along the coast.

   c Wave action is eroding the land.

   d The council has to keep coastal defences repaired.

   e People will bring their swimming costumes and towels when they visit.

   f Biological weathering is occurring.

   g The land may flood during storms.

   h The rocks are more resistant to erosion.

   i Caves may form.

   j Visitors will come to see the sea views.

2. Write down all the things you have learned to do in this unit. You can find some ideas in the help box – but not all of them are right!

3. Look again at the five geographical questions you asked at the beginning of this unit. Are they the same as any given below? Can you answer them all now?

   ⊚ What is weathering?

   ⊚ What is erosion?

   ⊚ How do waves shape the coast?

   ⊚ How does the sea erode the coast?

   ⊚ What features are found around the coast?

   ⊚ Why do cliffs collapse?

   ⊚ How can we manage our coasts?

help!

Research	Asking geographical questions
Writing in persuasion genre	Drawing sketch maps
Writing in report genre	Working with others
Writing in explanation genre	Using map contour lines
Annotating diagrams	Using an atlas

3 Shopping – past, present and future

A Shopping on the Internet

B Shopping centre in Kingston upon Thames

C Out-of-town shopping, Rubery, Birmingham

D Market stall in London

E Shopping street in Liverpool

Learn about

Shopping has become an important aspect of the lives of people in MEDCs. Everybody shops! But how and where people shop has changed and is still changing. In this unit you will focus on the UK and learn about:

- where people shop for goods and services
- how shopping has changed and is changing now
- how changes in shopping affect different groups of people
- how to manage change in shopping.

F Corner shop in Lavenham, Suffolk

Setting the scene

G

Activities

1 a Study collage **G** above. Classify the goods you see into the categories *Necessities* (things people need) and *Luxuries* (things people want but do not need). Write them in a table like this:

Necessities	Luxuries
Potatoes	CDs

b Were all the goods easy to classify? If not, explain why some were difficult.

2 Now classify the goods into two categories that you have chosen yourself.

3 Study photographs **A–F**, which show different shopping environments. Put the photographs in order of:

a date (oldest to newest shopping environment)

b degree of activity (busy to quiet)

c atmosphere

d attractiveness

e personal associations (most familiar to least familiar).

Share your lists with the whole class. Justify the orders you have chosen.

4 a There are many different ways of shopping. In a group, make a list of all the ways you can think of.

b Use your list and the photographs to create two spider diagrams, one for *Shopping before 1900* and another for *Shopping today*. Some ways of shopping may go on both diagrams.

5 **Extension**

a Using photographs **A–F**, make a list of key words that describe shopping.

b Use your key words to complete this word puzzle.

Shopping **s**treets **s**ell **s**ausages, **s**hoes, **s**andwiches.

H
O
P
P
I
N
G

c Create your own word puzzle about shopping.

6 Begin a geography word bank for this unit.

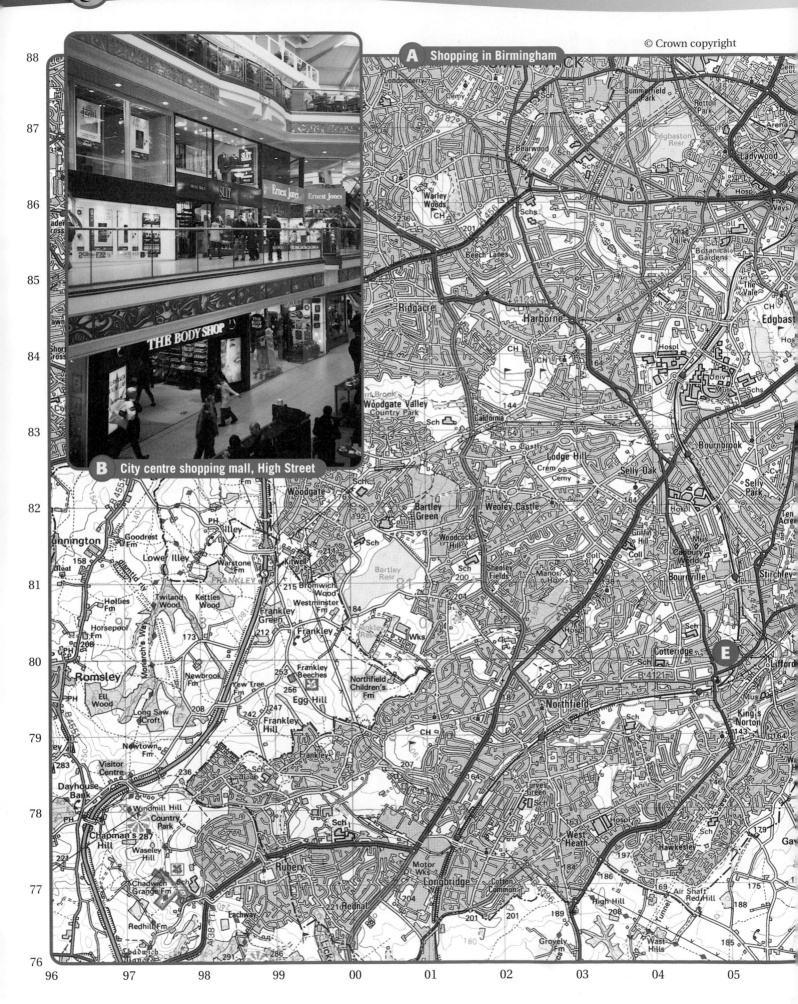

A Shopping in Birmingham

B City centre shopping mall, High Street

C City centre shopping street: New Street

Birmingham is the second largest city in England. It has many different types of shopping areas. The city centre is the largest shopping area in Birmingham, and local corner shops are the smallest. The number of shops, particularly local shops, in Birmingham is decreasing. However, over half of all the money spent on shopping in Birmingham is still spent in local shops.

People in Birmingham spend an average of £2500 per year each on **retail goods**. Spending on **convenience goods** went up by 6 per cent and spending on **comparison goods** by 46 per cent between 1994 and 1996.

D Suburban shopping street: Kings Heath

E Suburban corner shop: Cotteridge

Getting Technical ▾

⊚ **Convenience goods:** Goods that are needed every day, such as bread, milk and newspapers. They are often regarded as necessities.

⊚ **Comparison goods:** Goods that are regarded as luxuries, such as furniture, televisions, stereos and clothes.

⊚ **Shopping hierarchy:** When shops are put into an order based upon size or the type of good or service they provide.

⊚ **Sphere of influence:** The distance people are prepared to travel to use a shopping centre.

Activities

① a Study map **A**, which shows different shopping areas in Birmingham.

b In pairs, consider each shopping area and think about:

⊚ what sights you would see ⊚ what you would smell

⊚ what sounds you would hear ⊚ what textures you would see or feel.

② a In groups of three or four, discuss the advantages and disadvantages of the different types of shops.

b Copy and complete the table below for each of the photographs **B**, **C**, **D** and **E**.

Shopping area	Location	Goods sold	Advantages	Disadvantages
Shopping mall	City centre			

Shopping hierarchies

Shops can be grouped or classified into different categories. These can be based upon their size, upon the type of service or goods they provide or even upon the distance consumers are prepared to travel to visit them. One group could be small shops, which sell convenience goods such as food and newspapers – things which are needed every day. Another group could be large shops, which sell comparison goods like furniture or goods in bulk. These types of classifications can be organised into **shopping hierarchies**.

Type of shopping area	Frequency of visit	Type of goods/service	Sphere of influence
City centre shopping mall	Weekly/monthly	Specialist goods, mainly comparison	Up to 80 km
Out-of-town shopping centre	Weekly/monthly	Bulk buying, convenience/ comparison	Up to 30 km
Suburban shopping street	Two/three times a week	Mainly convenience	Local area
Corner shop	Daily	Mainly convenience	Neighbouring streets

A A shopping hierarchy

Activities

1 **a** Look at shopping hierarchy **A**. Now create a shopping hierarchy diagram for your own town or city. Add the names of actual places and shops or shopping centres to the first column.

  b By looking at shopping hierarchy **A**, try to explain *why* shopping malls are considered 'most important'.

  c Now look at your own shopping hierarchy. Explain why the shopping area you have put at the bottom of your hierarchy is the least important.

2 Compare and contrast two of the shopping areas in terms of their location, goods bought and frequency of use. You may want to use the comparison writing frame to help structure your writing. 📖

> Shops at ... and ... have similarities and differences.
>
> They are different in that ...   Also ... Another way they differ is that ...
>
> However, they are similar ... In the same way ... So ...

What's your rating?

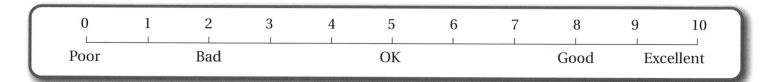

0	1	2	3	4	5	6	7	8	9	10
Poor		Bad			OK			Good		Excellent

Performance standards are an important part of evaluation. Schools, hospitals and railways are measured against performance standards to show how efficient they are. All around us, standards measure degrees of success. You are going to create and use a performance standard to evaluate shopping areas near you.

Activities

1 a These factors could be used to create a performance standard for shopping areas. In pairs, discuss the meaning and importance of each factor.

- Access
- Choice of shops
- Facilities for children, e.g. créche
- Seating areas

- Parking
- Toilets
- Facilities for disabled people

b Try to think of two extra factors to add to the list.

2 a Think of an example of each type of shopping area near where you live. Rate it by giving it a score from 1 to 10 for each factor in your performance standard. You can use a copy of the table below to help you. Add your own factors in the two empty columns.

Shopping area type	Name	Access	Parking	Choice	Toilets	Children	Disabled	Seating		
Corner shop										
Shopping street										
City centre shopping mall										
Out-of-town shopping										

b Which shopping centre do you rate as the best? Justify your choice.

c Now work out the mean (average) score for each shopping area. Rank them from highest to lowest score.

d Look back at your answer to **b**. Compare it to your answer to **c**. Do you think your performance standard gives a useful result? If not, suggest ways that you could change it to make it work better.

3 Do you think that all the factors are equally important? Choose the two most important and the two least important factors. Discuss your choice with your partner, and justify your decisions.

Different shoppers have different needs

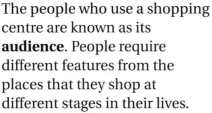

The people who use a shopping centre are known as its **audience**. People require different features from the places that they shop at different stages in their lives.

Activity

4 **a** Assess each type of shopping centre in activity **2** according to the individual needs of *one* of the following groups of people:

- young people
- people who live alone
- elderly people
- mothers with young children
- people without a car.

Look at photographs **A–D** to help you.

b Explain which shopping centre is best for the group of people you chose. Use the How to ... box to help you explain your choice of shopping centre.

How to ...

... write an explanation

Your explanation should be split into three sections:

1 **Thesis:** an opening statement or theory – say which shopping centre you think was best

2 **Argument:** arguments and evidence to support your thesis – say *why* you thought it was the best

3 **Summary:** a summary supporting the opening statement.

How has shopping changed?

Case Study: Poplar Road, Kings Heath, Birmingham

Poplar Road in 1904

1904

4	George Atkins	*Glass and china dealer*
6	Miss Selina Clark	*Sweets*
8	Joseph Findon	*Fried fish*
10	Arthur Taylor	*Musical instruments*
12	Charles Cooper	*Tailor*
14	Charles Parkes	*Hairdresser*
16	Robert Guest	*Plumber*
20	Frederick Gel	*Furniture maker*
28	Thomas Farren	*Butcher*
30	Richard Allen	*Painter*
34	Albert Gell	*Furniture maker*
36	William Armishaw	*Painter and Decorator*
38	William Philpott	*Laundry owner*
40	Albert Spiers	*Cycle dealer*
42	Henry Humphreys	*Ironmonger, glass and china*
44	John Barclay	*Manager, Cooperative Society*
46	John Bluck	*China and glass dealer*

A From *Kelly's Directory of Birmingham*, 1904

B Shops in Poplar Road, 1992

4	**Off Limits** Compact Discs		32	**Poplar Restaurant** Restaurant
6	**Lady Di** Shoes		34	**Delta** Stationery
8	**Sarah's** Delicatessen		36	**Poplar Café** Teas and Snacks
10	**Childsplay** Toys		38	**Clive Mark** School uniform
12	**Valerie Rudd** Handbags		40	Empty
14	**Pollyannas** Lace		42	**Smart Gear** Clothes
16	**AA Jewellery** Jewellery and Giftware		44	Empty
18–30	**Safeway** Supermarket and car park			

1992

C Shops and businesses in Poplar Road, 2001

4	**The Glory Hole** Catalogue clearance		16	**Jewellers and Repairs** Jewellery and giftware
6	**AJ's** Hairdresser		18–30	**Safeway** Supermarket and car park
8	Empty			
10	**Childsplay** Toys		32	**Los Caracores** Mediterranean restaurant
12	**Caribbean Sam** Caribbean food		34	**Gas Line** Cookers, fires, fridges
14	**Armadillo** Clothes and gifts		36	Empty
			38–40	**Clive Mark** School uniform
			42	**Mann & Co** Solicitors
			44	Empty

2001

Poplar Road in 2001

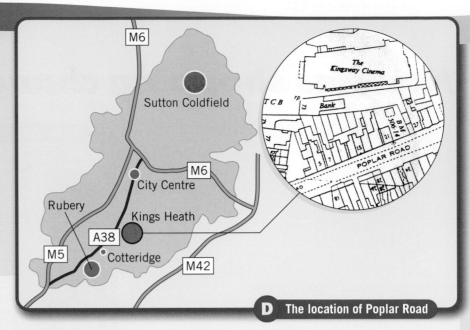

D The location of Poplar Road

Activities

1 Look at the photographs and information on Poplar Road.
Decide in which year people were most likely to:

a buy a glass vase

b buy milk at 7.30 pm

c get a cup of tea

d buy many different types of products in the same shop

e order fresh meat for Christmas.

2 a Read the data on shop types in **A**, **B** and **C** again. Think of four headings you could use to classify the shops.

b Write the shops in 1904, 1992 and 2000 under your headings. You could set up a database to sort and compare this data. **ICT**

3 a In pairs, discuss how the shops on Poplar Road changed between 1904 and 2000.

b Try to think of three reasons for these changes.

c Share your reasons with another pair of students.

4 Describe and explain the changing shop types in Poplar Road. In your answer you should describe *how* the shopping types have changed over time. Then explain *why* some factors, like accessibility, have become more important, while other factors may have become less important.

You could start your *description* like this:

> The types of shops on Poplar Road have changed over the past hundred years. In 1904 ...

Your *explanation* could start:

> People's shopping habits have changed since 1904 because ... This means that in Poplar Road ...

5 **Extension**

Use fieldwork and a historical directory from your local library to investigate changing shopping patterns in your local area.

What is the future of shopping?

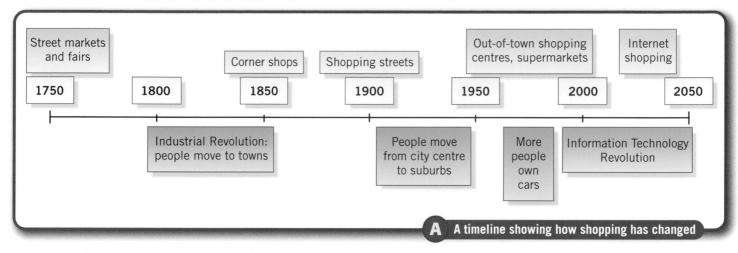

A A timeline showing how shopping has changed

During the Industrial Revolution in the early nineteenth century, many more people started to live and work in towns. They needed shops to provide the goods, particularly food, that in the country they produced themselves. In the present-day Information Technology Revolution, advances in technology and telecommunications have changed the way people live and work – and how and where they shop. People no longer have to carry cash because they can buy goods using plastic cards – they can even buy goods without leaving their homes. In 2001, more than three-quarters of people in the UK did some of their shopping from home, either by post, telephone or over the Internet. The long-term future of shopping is uncertain – how will people shop in the year 2050?

Activity

1 a Find three websites that sell goods or services that you can also buy in a shop. You can find web addresses in newspaper advertisements or by using a search engine. **ICT**

  b List five ways in which shopping using the Internet is different from shopping in shops.

help!

Compare the two types of shopping by considering these questions:

⚙ What do you buy?

⚙ How do you pay?

⚙ How accessible is it?

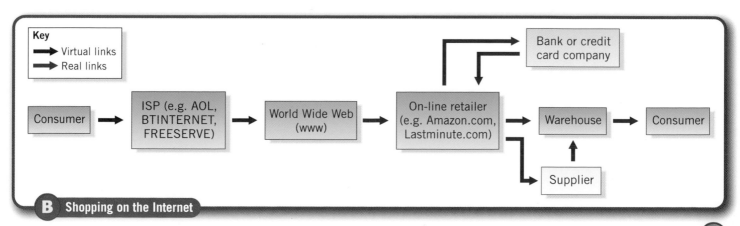

B Shopping on the Internet

Activities

2 Shopping in shops and shopping via the Internet are *Parallel Shopping Worlds*. In groups of four, copy and complete the table to show the positive and negative aspects of shopping in these two ways.

	Shopping in shops	Internet shopping
Positive aspects		
Negative aspects		

3 In your groups, consider what the effects would be if goods were only available via the Internet.

4 Draw and annotate a cartoon or picture of how you think people will shop in 2050.

help!

Think about the impacts on:
- the built environment
- social relationships (meeting people)
- transport
- employment
- consumer choice
- prices of goods
- access to technology
- control of purchases.

5 Imagine you are responsible for marketing a product on the Internet.

a Design a web page advertising the product you have chosen. You could use a desktop publishing package to help you. (ICT)

b You have been asked to make a presentation to your company to explain how you are marketing the product. Use the prompts in the help box to structure your presentation.

6 Think about the changes in shopping identified in this unit. Write an account titled: *How and why has shopping changed? How is it likely to change in the future?*

Your account should have three sections:
- **Situation**: the background to changes in shopping
- **Events**: more detail on the changes in shopping
- **Outcome**: closing statement to sum up and predict the future.

help!

Remember to consider all aspects of marketing your product:

- **Product** – what is it?
  - what is it made of?
  - does it have any special features?
- **Promotion** – where is it going to be advertised?
  - any special offers?
- **Price** – how much can you charge? Your price must be low enough to make people want to buy, but remember: you need to make a profit!
- **Place** – where is your product made or stored?
  - how will it reach the customer?

Review and reflect

A question of shopping

Activities

1. You are used to giving answers to questions. For some questions there is only one correct answer, but for others there may be a number of answers. In pairs, try to think of suitable questions for each of the answers below. They can be in the form of puzzles, problems, diagrams or written questions.

   a Technological innovation.

   b Convenience goods.

   c Located mainly in the city centre.

   d The young and the elderly.

   e Home shopping – especially using the Internet.

   f Weekly.

   g Local corner shops at the bottom of the hierarchy.

   h Out-of-town shopping centres.

   i Changes in shopping patterns over 20–30 years.

2. Share your questions with another pair.

3. **Extension**

   Think up some more answers from this unit.
   Ask your partner to think of the questions.

4 Weather patterns over Europe

A Satellite image of Europe, 18 July 1999

Learn about

Weather is the condition of the atmosphere. It affects most people's lives every day. Many people need to understand the weather to do their jobs. In this unit you will learn about:

- weather and climate patterns and processes in Europe
- reading weather maps and satellite images
- how to forecast the weather
- the difference between weather and climate
- drawing and reading climate graphs
- how to choose a holiday destination with a climate that suits your family.

What is Europe like?

Activities

① Maps use words, colours, lines and symbols to show information about places. Look at **B**, which is a **political map** of Europe. There are a number of different types of line on this political map – *coastlines, national (country) boundaries* and *lines of latitude and longitude*. Which of these lines can actually be seen on the surface of the Earth?

② Use the contents page of an atlas to find a **physical map** of Europe. Now write four lists giving the different types of information that a physical map shows as words, colours, lines and symbols.

③ **a** Which lines on the physical map can actually be seen on the surface of the Earth?

b Which lines cannot be seen?

help!

✪ A **political map** shows countries and their main cities, including the capital.

✪ A **physical map** shows information about the natural features on the Earth's surface, such as rivers, mountains and oceans.

④ Now look at the satellite image **A** of Europe on the opposite page.

a What information does this show that can also be seen on political or physical maps?

b What information is shown that would not appear on an atlas map?

c Why is this type of information not shown on atlas maps?

⑤ **a** Which countries on the satellite image have very little cloud cover?

b Name any countries that cannot be seen due to cloud cover.

What are clouds and why does it rain?

Clouds are made up of water droplets or ice crystals, depending upon how cold the surrounding air is. These are so small that they 'float' in the **atmosphere**. Clouds form when air cools so that the **water vapour** it holds condenses into water droplets. Clouds are classified by height and shape. There are three main cloud types.

- **Cirrus clouds** are made of ice crystals because they form high up in the atmosphere where temperatures are below freezing point.

- **Stratus clouds** form in a layer or 'sheet' across the sky and tend to be much lower in the atmosphere. They are called fog when they are at ground level.

- **Cumulus clouds** have 'bumpy' tops because of the rising air currents that create them. Sometimes **cumulonimbus clouds** form when air rises very quickly. They tend to be extremely tall.

Some cloud types, such as cirrus, never cause precipitation (rain, hail or snow). Others, like cumulonimbus, bring rain or hail with thunder and lightning. Clouds play an important part in the **hydrological cycle (D)**.

A Stratus clouds

B Cirrus clouds

C Cumulus clouds

The hydrological cycle

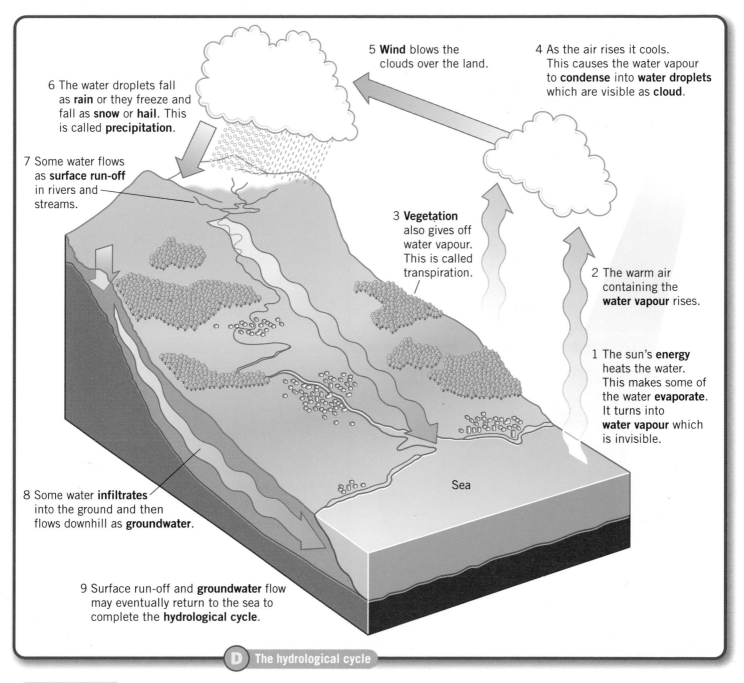

5 **Wind** blows the clouds over the land.

4 As the air rises it cools. This causes the water vapour to **condense** into **water droplets** which are visible as **cloud**.

6 The water droplets fall as **rain** or they freeze and fall as **snow** or **hail**. This is called **precipitation**.

7 Some water flows as **surface run-off** in rivers and streams.

3 **Vegetation** also gives off water vapour. This is called transpiration.

2 The warm air containing the **water vapour** rises.

1 The sun's **energy** heats the water. This makes some of the water **evaporate**. It turns into **water vapour** which is invisible.

8 Some water **infiltrates** into the ground and then flows downhill as **groundwater**.

9 Surface run-off and **groundwater** flow may eventually return to the sea to complete the **hydrological cycle**.

Sea

D The hydrological cycle

Activities

1 Create a word bank for all the terms in **bold** print on pages 48 and 49, including those in diagram **D** above. You may remember some of them from *Geography Matters 1*.

2 Write a story about a water molecule called H_2O travelling around the hydrological cycle. Try to use most of the geographical vocabulary in your word bank. Use the numbers for each annotation on diagram **D** to help you sequence your story correctly. You could begin your story like this ...

> One day H_2O, a water molecule, was warming himself in the heat of the midday sun when he began to disappear. Suddenly he saw the sea below him and realised he must have <u>evaporated</u> and turned into ...

What causes cloud and rain?

Clouds form when air rises and cools so that the water vapour it holds condenses into droplets. Air can be forced to rise in three different ways to give three types of precipitation: **convectional**, **relief** and **frontal**. It rains when the water droplets become too large and heavy to stay up in the air.

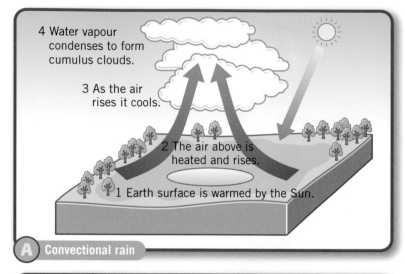

4 Water vapour condenses to form cumulus clouds.

3 As the air rises it cools.

2 The air above is heated and rises.

1 Earth surface is warmed by the Sun.

A Convectional rain

Convectional rain

When the Earth's surface is heated by the Sun, the air above it is also warmed up. The warm air rises but as it rises it cools down. As the air cools the water vapour it holds condenses and clouds form. Eventually it may rain. If the air rises very quickly cumulonimbus storm clouds may form. **Convectional rain** often happens in Europe during hot summer weather.

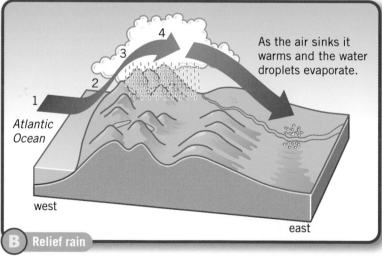

As the air sinks it warms and the water droplets evaporate.

Atlantic Ocean

west

east

B Relief rain

Relief rain

Relief means the shape of the land. When air is forced to rise over mountains it cools and the water vapour it holds condenses to form clouds. Eventually **relief rain** may fall. European weather comes mainly from the Atlantic Ocean and moves towards the east. This means that a lot of the moisture held in the air will fall on the mountains in Western Europe. By the time the air reaches Eastern Europe much of the moisture will already have fallen so there tends to be less rain.

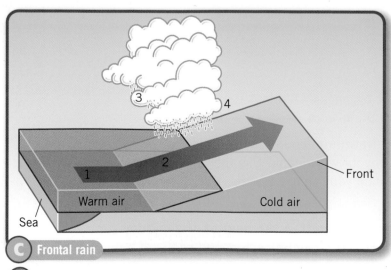

Warm air

Cold air

Sea

Front

C Frontal rain

Frontal rain

Warm air is lighter than cold air. When the two meet, the warmer air rises over the colder, heavier air. As the warm air is forced to rise it cools, so that the water vapour it holds condenses to form clouds. The zone where warm air and cold air meet is called a *front*. On a weather map a cold front looks like this: ▲▲▲ and a warm front like this: ●●● . In Europe, bands of cloud and rain are often found along fronts.

D Satellite image of Europe for 18 July 1999

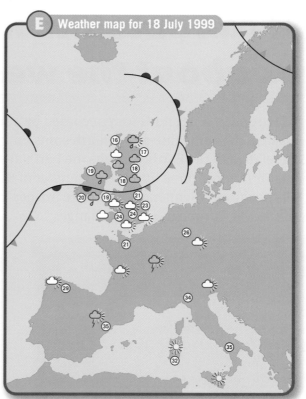

E Weather map for 18 July 1999

Activities

1 Diagram **A** has been labelled to explain how convectional rain forms. Use this to help you to match the sentences below to the numbers on diagram **B** for relief rain.

- As the air rises, it cools and the water vapour it holds condenses to form clouds.
- Air continues to rise until relief rainfall occurs.
- Moist, warm air blows from the Atlantic Ocean.
- The air is forced to rise over the mountains of Western Europe.

2 Use your answers to activity **1** to help you write four labels explaining how frontal rainfall is formed in **C**.

3 Look carefully at satellite image **D** – you can see a larger version on page 46. For each area of cloud labelled **a–e**:

a Describe its location (where it is found).

b Say whether you think it was formed by convection, relief or at a front. Compare the satellite image to the weather map **E** and physical map **F** to help you to decide.

4 Which type of cloud and rainfall (convectional, relief or frontal) tends to affect the largest area of Europe at any one time?

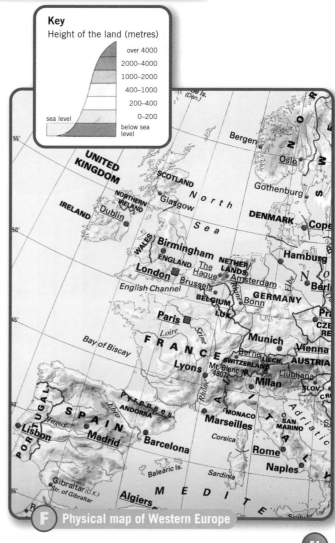

Key
Height of the land (metres)

	over 4000
	2000–4000
	1000–2000
	400–1000
	200–400
sea level	0–200
	below sea level

F Physical map of Western Europe

What can satellite images tell us about the weather?

The images of Europe in **A**, **D** and **G** were recorded by a satellite called METEOSAT. It goes around the Earth at the same rate as the Earth spins on its axis. This means that it stays in the same position relative to the Earth. It orbits the Earth at a height of about 35 000 kilometres above the Equator (almost three times the diameter of the Earth). It can image almost half the Earth from this position. A sequence of satellite images like those on this page can show how weather patterns over Europe move and change.

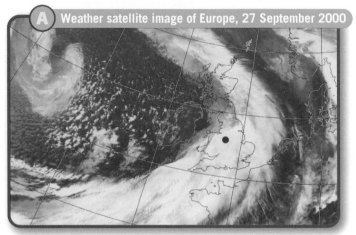
A Weather satellite image of Europe, 27 September 2000

B Weather over Chester, 27 September 2000

D Weather satellite image of Europe, 28 September 2000

E Weather over Chester, 28 September 2000

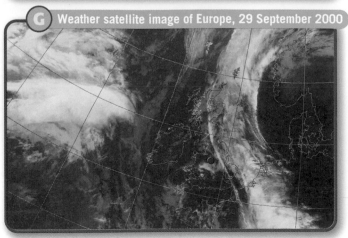
G Weather satellite image of Europe, 29 September 2000

H Weather over Chester, 29 September 2000

Key
● Location of Chester

Satellite images provide weather forecasters with essential information. For example, they can be used to track storms and warn people who may be affected by them. Many people, such as workers on oil rigs and in power stations, farmers and ferry operators, rely on satellite images to inform them about the weather.

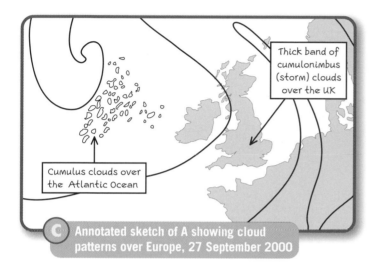

Thick band of cumulonimbus (storm) clouds over the UK

Cumulus clouds over the Atlantic Ocean

C Annotated sketch of A showing cloud patterns over Europe, 27 September 2000

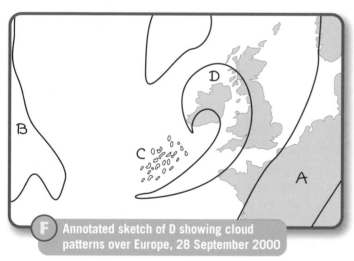

D

B

C

A

F Annotated sketch of D showing cloud patterns over Europe, 28 September 2000

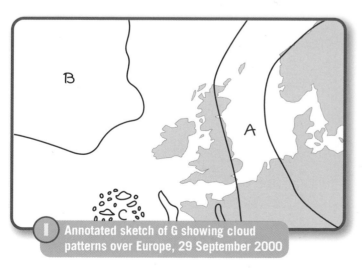

B

A

C

I Annotated sketch of G showing cloud patterns over Europe, 29 September 2000

Activities

Figure **C** is an annotated sketch of satellite image **A**. The annotations describe the cloud patterns and their locations over Europe. Use it as a guide to help you do activities **1** and **2**. You can see the different cloud types on page 48.

1 Match the annotations below to letters **A–D** on sketch **F**.

- Cumulus clouds to the south-west of Ireland.
- Thin stratus cloud over the Atlantic Ocean.
- A band of cumulonimbus cloud over Spain, France and Scandinavia.
- A 'swirl' of thick cloud to the west of the UK and France.

2 Use your answers to activity **1** to write annotations for the areas lettered **A–C** on sketch **I**. Include the location of the cloud.

3 Europe's weather usually comes from one main direction. Look at the sequence of weather patterns shown in images **A**, **D** and **G** and suggest which direction this is.

4 Look at photographs **B**, **E** and **H** and the satellite images recorded at the same times. How do clouds look different when viewed from above and from below?

5 Use the information on page 48 to name the main cloud types in photographs **B**, **E** and **H**.

6 **Extension** ICT

- **a** Download satellite images for the last three days by going to www.heinemann.co.uk/hotlinks (insert code 5171P).
- **b** Draw a sequence of dated sketch maps, like **C**, **F** and **I**, showing the weather patterns. Annotate the cloud patterns.

How can weather information be presented?

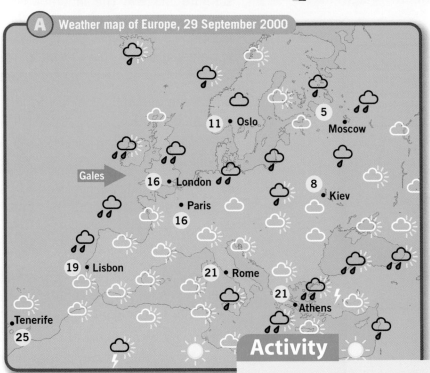

A Weather map of Europe, 29 September 2000

11 • Oslo
5 Moscow
Gales →
16 • London
• Paris
16
8 • Kiev
19 • Lisbon
21 • Rome
21 • Athens
•Tenerife
25

Meteorologists are people who study and **forecast** the weather. The information they use comes from weather stations, satellite images and computer models.

Map **A** shows the pattern of weather over Europe on 29 September 2000. Satellite image **G** on page 52 shows information for the same day.

Weather stations record a range of different aspects of the weather. Table **B** shows data from a weather station in Chester for the period 20–29 September 2000. Use the Getting Technical box to help you to understand the data shown.

Getting Technical

⊚ **Humidity**: the amount of water vapour held in the air, measured as a percentage. If the air is at 100 per cent humidity, it is likely to form clouds or be foggy.

⊚ **Wind speed**: how fast the air is moving measured in kilometres or miles per hour.

⊚ **Wind direction**: the compass direction *from* which the wind blows.

Activity

1 Work in pairs to compare the weather map for 29 September 2000 with the satellite image for the same day on page 52.

   a Write down five types of information which are shown on the map but not on the satellite image.

   b Write down three types of information which are shown on the satellite image but not on the map.

   c How can a sequence of weather maps and satellite images, for a number of days, help people to forecast the weather?

Date	Average temperature (°C)	Precipitation (mm)	Humidity (%)	Wind speed (kmph)	Wind direction
September 20	12	6	89	13	SE
September 21	17	0	78	8	S
September 22	17	0	77	5	S
September 23	18	0	78	6	S
September 24	12	11	89	14	SE
September 25	13	8	86	8	SE
September 26	14	7	88	8	SE
September 27	13	5	86	13	SE
September 28	16	1	81	10	S
September 29	14	2	83	8	SE

B Weather data for Chester for 20–29 September 2000

Geographical enquiry: How do different aspects of the weather affect each other?

Activities

1 **Asking geographical questions**

It is difficult to answer such a 'big' enquiry question without breaking it down into smaller questions such as: *How does temperature in Chester affect humidity?* Suggest three more smaller questions you can investigate using only the data in table **B**.

2 **Collecting information**

You can find the data you need to carry out this enquiry in table **B**. If you want to improve your geographical skills, try to collect your own set of weather data and use it to carry out a similar enquiry (see extension activity **6**).

> **ICT idea** Enter the data in table **B** into a computer spreadsheet and then carry out the enquiry.

3 **Presenting data**

A scattergraph is one way of presenting data which shows if there is any correlation (relationship) between two factors. For example, in figure **C** temperature has been plotted on the *X* axis and humidity on the *Y* axis. It shows that there is a **negative correlation** between temperature and humidity, i.e. *as temperature increases, humidity decreases*.

a Plot two more scattergraphs for:

◎ precipitation and humidity

◎ wind speed and temperature.

b Why can't you show data for wind direction on a scattergraph?

c Design a way of presenting this information to show whether it affects any other aspects of the weather shown in table **B**.

4 **Analysing data to form conclusions**

a For each of the graphs you have drawn, say whether it shows a *positive*, *negative* or *no* correlation.

b Write a sentence to describe each one, e.g. *As temperature increases, humidity decreases*.

c Give reasons for the type of correlation shown in each graph.

5 **Forecasting the weather**

Look back at the sequence of satellite images on page 52 and the weather data in table **B** for the same three days. Use this information and the results of your weather enquiry to complete this weather forecast for 30 September in Chester. Choose the correct word from each pair in *italics*.

> Tomorrow will see the front currently over the Atlantic Ocean moving *west / east* across the British Isles. This will bring *thick cumulus / high cirrus* cloud and heavy showers to the Chester area. There will be a *few / long* sunny spells. As a result the average temperature will *increase / decrease* to around *12°C / 16°C* and the humidity will *increase / decrease* to about 88 per cent. Wind speeds are likely to *increase / decrease* to about 13 km per hour.

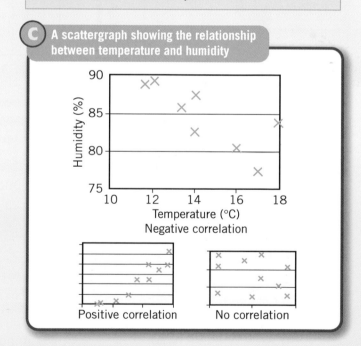

C A scattergraph showing the relationship between temperature and humidity

6 **Extension**

Use weather data from a school or local weather station, plus weather maps from a local newspaper, to carry out a similar enquiry.

You can download recent satellite images from weather websites at www.heinemann.co.uk/hotlinks (insert code 5171P).

What types of climate does Europe have?

So far this unit has focused on the weather. Weather is the short-term or day-to-day state of the atmosphere in a place. Climate, on the other hand, is the average pattern of weather for an area taken over many years (usually 30 years). Europe is large enough to have several different types of climate (see **F** opposite).

Average monthly temperature and precipitation data for a place can be shown on a climate graph like **A**, which shows information for Valencia, Ireland. The red line shows the average temperature, measured in degrees Celsius, for each month – use the left-hand vertical axis to read off the values. The blue bars show the average rainfall or precipitation, measured in millimetres, for each month – read the values off the right-hand vertical axis.

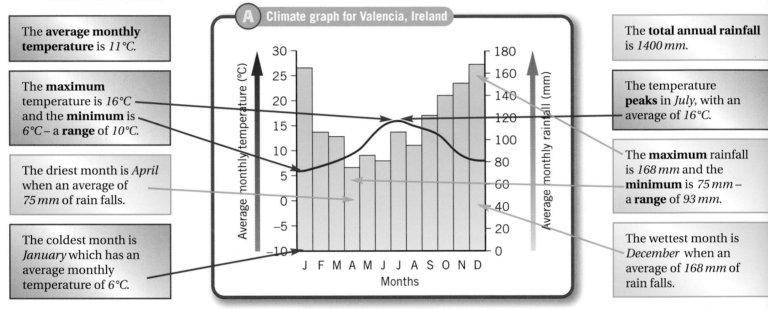

A Climate graph for Valencia, Ireland

The **average monthly temperature** is *11°C*.

The **maximum** temperature is *16°C* and the **minimum** is *6°C* – a **range** of *10°C*.

The driest month is *April* when an average of *75 mm* of rain falls.

The coldest month is *January* which has an average monthly temperature of *6°C*.

The **total annual rainfall** is *1400 mm*.

The temperature **peaks** in *July*, with an average of *16°C*.

The **maximum** rainfall is *168 mm* and the **minimum** is *75 mm* – a **range** of *93 mm*.

The wettest month is *December* when an average of *168 mm* of rain falls.

Getting Technical ▼

- Ⓖ **Annual** – yearly
- Ⓖ **Total annual rainfall** – to calculate this, add up rainfall over all twelve months
- Ⓖ **Average monthly temperature** – to calculate this, add up each monthly temperature and divide by 12 (months)
- Ⓖ **Maximum** – the highest amount
- Ⓖ **Minimum** – the lowest amount
- Ⓖ **Peak** – the highest point in a graph or trend line
- Ⓖ **Range** – the difference between the lowest and the highest amounts

Activities ①②③

① Table **B** shows the climate data for Lisbon in Portugal. Draw a climate graph, using the one in **A** to help you.

	J	F	M	A	M	J	J	A	S	O	N	D
Average monthly temperature (°C)	11	12	14	16	17	20	22	23	21	18	14	12
Average monthly rainfall (mm)	111	76	109	54	44	16	3	4	33	62	93	103

B

② Annotate your climate graph with boxes of text, using **A** to guide you. In most cases you will only need to change the *data* or the *month* – you can use the same wording. Look at the Getting Technical box if you need help.

③ Shade in the annotation boxes that describe the rainfall in blue, and those that describe the temperature in red.

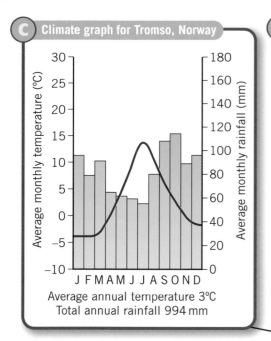

C Climate graph for Tromso, Norway

Average annual temperature 3°C
Total annual rainfall 994 mm

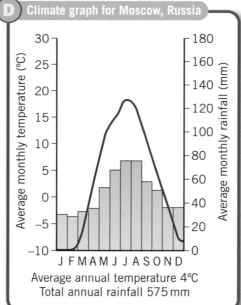

D Climate graph for Moscow, Russia

Average annual temperature 4°C
Total annual rainfall 575 mm

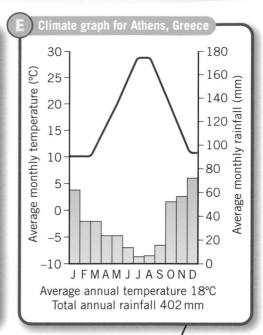

E Climate graph for Athens, Greece

Average annual temperature 18°C
Total annual rainfall 402 mm

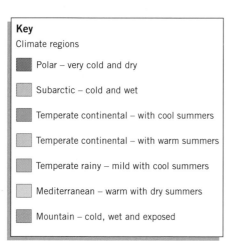

Key

Climate regions

- Polar – very cold and dry
- Subarctic – cold and wet
- Temperate continental – with cool summers
- Temperate continental – with warm summers
- Temperate rainy – mild with cool summers
- Mediterranean – warm with dry summers
- Mountain – cold, wet and exposed

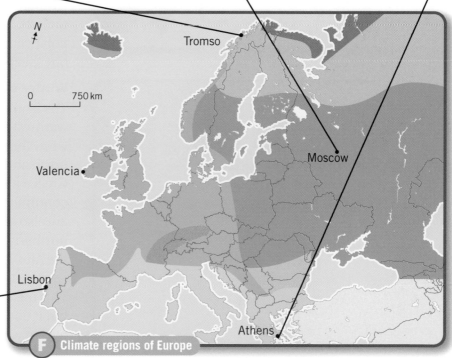

N

0   750 km

Tromso

Moscow

Valencia

Lisbon

Athens

F Climate regions of Europe

Activities

1. For each of the five places marked on **F**, name the climate region in which it is located.

2. **a** Rank the five places marked on **F** according to their average annual temperatures. Rank them from highest to lowest temperature.

   b Do average temperatures generally increase or decrease as you go north in Europe?

3. **a** Rank the five places from highest to lowest annual rainfall totals.

   b Do rainfall totals generally increase or decrease as you go east across Europe?

4. **a** Calculate the temperature ranges for each of the five places in **F**.

   b Rank the five places from highest to lowest temperature ranges.

   c Do temperature ranges generally increase or decrease as you go east across Europe?

5. **Extension**

   Work in pairs to try to identify any other climate patterns across Europe.

What affects Europe's climate?

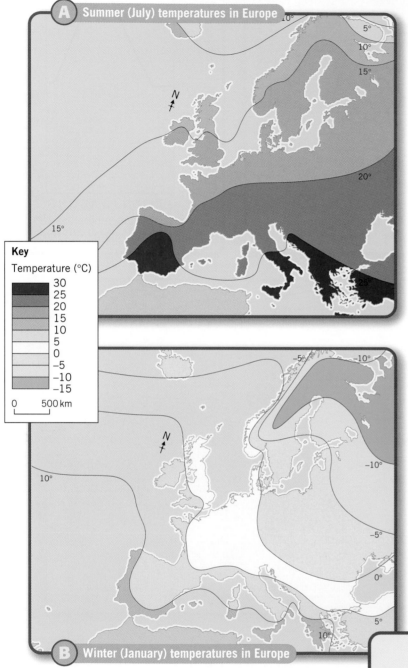

A **Summer (July) temperatures in Europe**

Key
Temperature (°C)

	30
	25
	20
	15
	10
	5
	0
	−5
	−10
	−15

0   500 km

B **Winter (January) temperatures in Europe**

Temperatures in Europe

Lines on maps which join places with equal temperatures are called **isotherms**.

Summer temperatures

The isotherms for July show that temperatures are highest in southern Europe and that they decrease as you go northwards. This variation across Europe affects many things, such as the types of plants that grow wild or on farms. In southern Europe, where there is a Mediterranean climate, crops such as olives, grapes and citrus fruits can be grown. High temperatures also attract large numbers of tourists. In northern Europe, where there is a polar climate, it is too cold for crops to ripen but sheep and reindeer can be reared.

Winter temperatures

The isotherms for January show that the warmest areas of Europe are in the south and west. Temperatures decrease towards the north and east. In southern Spain, Italy and Greece it is warm enough for farming to continue through the winter. Many tourists are also attracted by the warm weather. In northern Europe and mountainous areas like the Alps and Pyrenees it is cold enough for snow to lie on the ground for many months. This means that farming cannot take place, but it does attract tourists who want to take part in winter sports.

Factors that affect temperature

Altitude

Temperatures decrease by about 1°C for every 100 metres increase in height above sea level. Many parts of the Alps are over 4000 metres above sea level, which means they are about 40°C colder than the coastal area to the south.

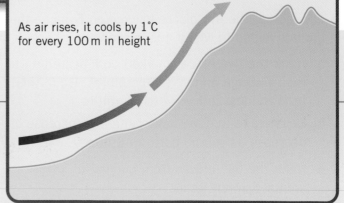

As air rises, it cools by 1°C for every 100 m in height

Latitude

Places near the Equator are warmer than places near the poles. This is due to the angle at which the Sun's rays hit the Earth's curved surface.

In southern Europe the Sun is at a higher angle so that its rays are concentrated on a small area of the Earth's surface. Towards the North Pole the Sun shines on the Earth's curved surface at a lower angle. This means its heat is spread over a larger area so that temperatures are lower.

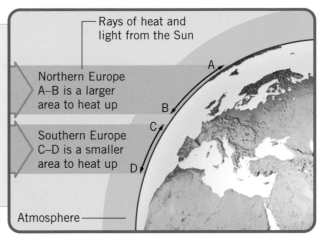

Rays of heat and light from the Sun

Northern Europe A–B is a larger area to heat up

Southern Europe C–D is a smaller area to heat up

Atmosphere

Distance from the sea

Solids heat up much quicker than liquids, so in summer land areas are warmer than the sea. However, solids also cool down quicker than liquids, so in winter the sea tends to be warmer than the land. This means that the distance a place is from the sea affects its temperature:

• in summer, places on coasts are cooler than places inland

• in winter, places on coasts are warmer than places inland.

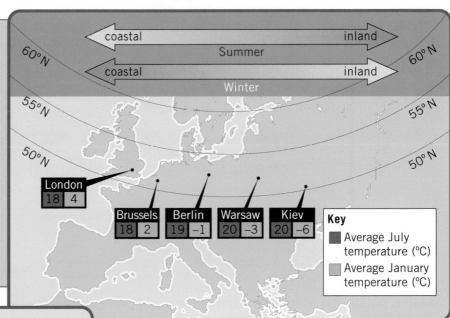

coastal   inland
Summer
coastal   inland
Winter

London
18 | 4

Brussels
18 | 2

Berlin
19 | –1

Warsaw
20 | –3

Kiev
20 | –6

Key
Average July temperature (°C)
Average January temperature (°C)

Ocean currents

The North Atlantic Drift is a warm current of water that flows across the Atlantic Ocean from the Gulf of Mexico. It keeps the coasts of western Europe much warmer than areas inland.

Prevailing winds

The prevailing wind is the direction from which the wind blows most often. For most of Europe the prevailing wind is from the south-west. The temperature of a prevailing wind is affected by the area it blows over. Prevailing winds bring:

• warm weather to western Europe when they blow over the warm North Atlantic Drift

• warm weather when they blow over the land in summer or the sea in winter

• cool weather if they blow over the land in winter or the cooler sea areas in summer.

Key
Ocean currents
warm
cool
Prevailing winds
summer
winter

0   500 km

North Atlantic Drift

Precipitation in Europe

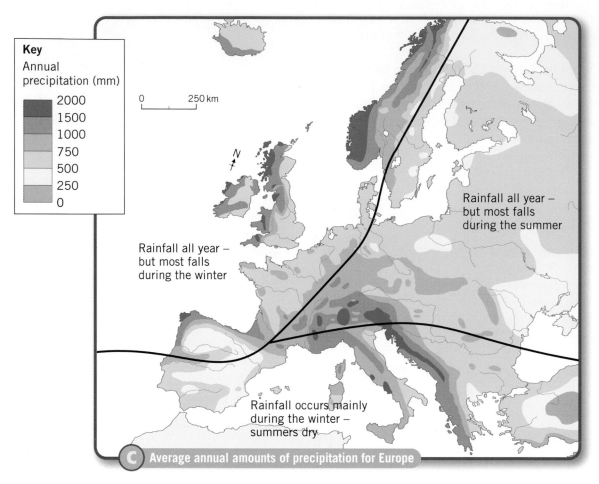

Key
Annual precipitation (mm)

- 2000
- 1500
- 1000
- 750
- 500
- 250
- 0

0   250 km

N

Rainfall all year – but most falls during the summer

Rainfall all year – but most falls during the winter

Rainfall occurs mainly during the winter – summers dry

C Average annual amounts of precipitation for Europe

Map **C** shows the average annual amounts of precipitation for Europe. It shows two main patterns:

1   Precipitation is higher where there are mountains, such as the Alps and the Apennines in Italy. This is due to *relief rainfall* (see diagram **B** on on page 50).

2   Precipitation is generally highest in the west and decreases towards the east. This is because **prevailing winds** bring moist air from the Atlantic Ocean. This causes either *frontal rainfall* (see diagram **C** on page 50) or *relief rainfall* as the air rises from sea level over the land. As the air moves eastwards it loses its moisture as precipitation. This means that eastern Europe usually has a drier climate.

Precipitation falls at different times of the year across different parts of Europe.

- **North-west Europe** receives precipitation throughout the year, but there tends to be more in winter than in summer.

- **Eastern Europe** receives precipitation throughout the year, but it tends to be highest in summer. This is because of *convectional rain* caused by high temperatures (see diagram A on page 50).

- **Mediterranean Europe** receives most of its rainfall in winter and the summers are usually dry.

Precipitation and human activities

Some parts of Mediterranean Europe experience **drought** as a result of a lack of precipitation during the summer months. Farmers' crops may die and water supplies for homes and industry are affected. When precipitation does occur, it is often as convectional rainfall. This tends to be heavy and can cause flooding or soil erosion, creating more problems for farmers. However, the dry summers attract tourists who spend a lot of money in some of Europe's poorest countries, such as Greece and Portugal.

In other parts of Europe, precipitation actually attracts tourists. Reliable snowfall in the Alps and Pyrenees brings millions of visitors seeking winter sports. Such precipitation does, however, interfere with farming, communications and industry.

D Soil erosion in Andalucia, Spain

Activities

① Copy table **E** below, which includes all the places marked on map **F** on page 62. Use the information in the maps on pages 47 (countries), 57 (climate types), 58 (temperatures in July and January) and 60 (rainfall) to complete the table. The information for Zermatt has been filled in for you.

Place	Country	Climate type	Average January temperature	Average July temperature	Average precipitation
Zermatt	Switzerland	mountain	0–5°C	20–25°C	1000–1500 mm
Bergen					
Odessa					
Moscow					
Kiruna					
Costa del Sol					

E

② For each of the descriptions below, work out the place in table **E** that it describes.

a Most of its precipitation comes in summer as convectional rainfall. Low winter temperatures are caused by the prevailing wind blowing across the cold land surface of Europe.

b Receives large amounts of relief and frontal rainfall throughout the year. It has mild winters because the prevailing winds blow over the warm North Atlantic Drift.

c The latitude of this place gives it high summer temperatures, while prevailing winds bring warm air from the Atlantic Ocean in winter.

d By the time the prevailing winds reach here they have already lost their moisture as frontal and relief rainfall. Its latitude causes it to have high summer temperatures.

e The latitude of this place accounts for its low temperatures all year round. Its distance from the warming effects of the Atlantic Ocean causes extremely low winter temperatures.

Where shall we go on holiday?

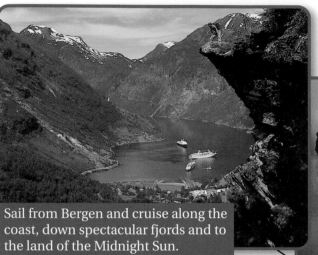

Sail from Bergen and cruise along the coast, down spectacular fjords and to the land of the Midnight Sun.

Stay in the Ice Hotel, Kiruna – built with 10 000 tonnes of crystal-clear ice.

Visit Moscow's famous Red Square and go to see the Bolshoi Ballet.

Ski in the shadow of the Matterhorn. Sample the *après-ski* as you relax by an open fire.

F Europe

The Crimea coastline has many beautiful resorts, splendid palaces and health spas.

Laze on the sandy beaches of Costa del Sol, shop till you drop then club all night long. Any energy left? ... Try paragliding or windsurfing!

Activity

③ Figure **F** shows the locations of the places named in table **E** on page 61, together with a brief description of the type of holiday you could experience there.

    a Look back at the climate details for each of the six places and then at **F**. Choose the place where you would most like to go on holiday. At which time of year would you go? Give your reasons why.

    b Choose a different holiday location on this page for a family member or a friend. At which time of year should they go? Why?

Review and reflect

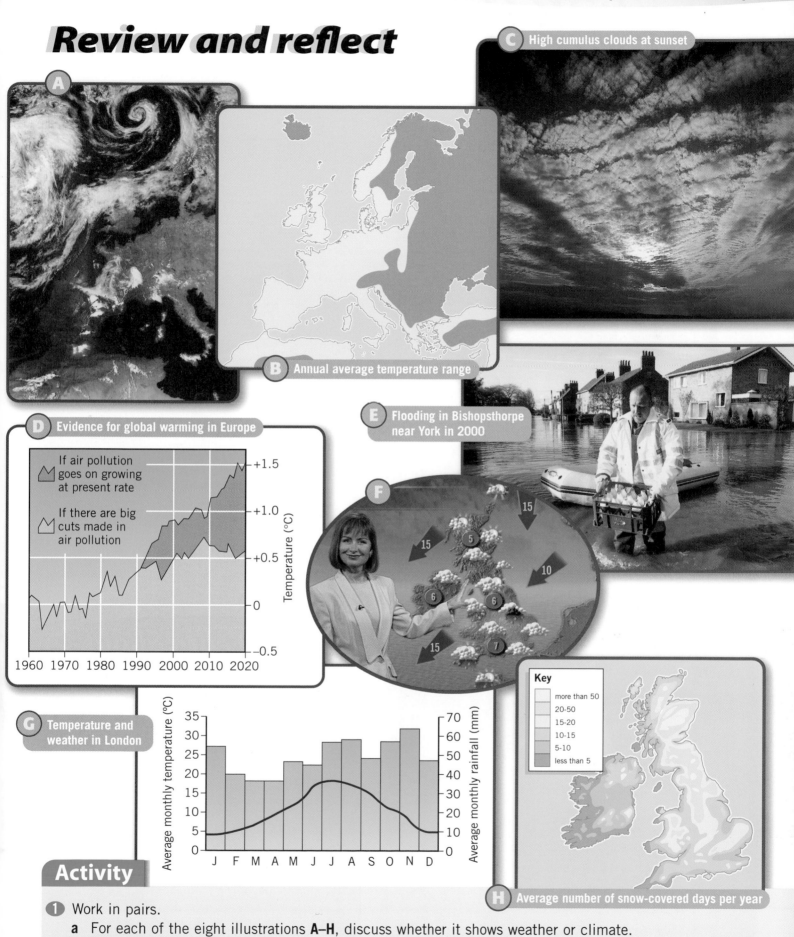

A

B Annual average temperature range

C High cumulus clouds at sunset

D Evidence for global warming in Europe

If air pollution goes on growing at present rate

If there are big cuts made in air pollution

E Flooding in Bishopsthorpe near York in 2000

F

G Temperature and weather in London

H Average number of snow-covered days per year

Key
more than 50
20-50
15-20
10-15
5-10
less than 5

Activity

1. Work in pairs.

   a For each of the eight illustrations **A–H**, discuss whether it shows weather or climate. Give reasons for your decisions.

   b Name the type of source shown in each case, e.g. *Source A is a satellite image of Europe.*

5 Investigating Brazil

A São Paulo, Brazil

B Itaipu hydroelectric dam, Brazil

Learn about

This unit is about Brazil. By the time you complete your work on Brazil you will have the skills to make a full investigation of any country in your future studies. You will investigate:

⊚ what it is like to live in Brazil

⊚ the location and scale of the country

⊚ different regions

⊚ whether Brazil is economically developed

⊚ what changes are occurring in the country

⊚ whether these changes have improved the lives of everybody in Brazil.

What do you know about Brazil?

Brazil is a wonderful country – it has everything to offer!

C Ipanema beach, Rio

Brazil is the fifth largest country in the world.

Brazil has the world's ninth largest economy.

There are over 163 million people in Brazil – Argentina, the next most populated South American country, only has 35 million.

Brazil is 8.5 million square kilometres in area. It is by far the largest country in South America.

Brazil has more forest than any other country.

What goes on in these high-rise buildings? Look closely at the photograph to find out whether they are office blocks or flats. Use the Internet to find names of companies which operate there.

What is the temperature? Use the climate maps in an atlas to find the temperatures experienced in Brazil.

D

Activities

1. Develop a brainstorm diagram to summarise what you already know about Brazil. The photographs opposite may help you to get started.

2. Look at photographs **A**, **B** and **C** in more detail. List all the geographical questions which could help you find out more about each of the pictures.

3. Suggest how you might start to answer the questions on your list. You could either set your work out in a table, or as labels on a sketch of the photograph (see **D**).

Questions you could ask	Possible way to find an answer
Where is this city located?	Refer to an atlas and find out where it is in Brazil.
How large is this city?	Use a more detailed reference atlas to find out the size of the city and its population.
What language is spoken there? Why?	Use an encyclopedia or textbook to find out about Brazil's past.

help!

- This activity is about how to carry out an investigation, so don't worry about the answers to your questions.
- Remember that nearly all geographical questions will include at least one of the words: *What? Where? Why? How? Who?*

Other images of Brazil

E Favela in São Paulo

Brazil fact file

- One per cent of landowners control over half the land in Brazil.
- The richest ten per cent of the population have an average income 78 times greater than the poorest ten per cent.
- Working conditions in some Brazilian factories are terrible.
- Production targets mean that many workers have to work twelve-hour shifts.
- The working week is often very long.
- Seven million Brazilian children are involved in child labour. They often do dangerous work for very low wages.

F Sandy river banks being eroded following deforestation in Para State, Amazonia

 Satellite image of South America

Key

 Andes Mountains

Tropical rainforest

Desert and semi-desert

Grassland and savannah

help!

Try to think about

⚙ stresses on the natural environment

⚙ economic stresses

⚙ social stresses.

Activities

④ Look carefully at photographs **E** and **F**. With a partner, list all the stresses on the environment that you can see in each of the pictures.

⑤ **Extension**

Try to find some more images of Brazil to add to your list of stresses. Look in other textbooks or try the Internet, for example, go to the geography page at the website listed on www.heinemann.co.uk/hotlinks (insert code 5171P).

⑥ Look back at the text and photographs on pages 64–67. Draw up a table of the positive and negative images that you associate with Brazil. Add the source of each image.

Positive images of Brazil	Negative images of Brazil
Smart high-rise buildings (source: photo A)	Poor housing (source: photo E)
Successful economy (source: text page 65)	

⑦ This activity is about **locating** photographs **A–C**, **E** and **F**.

a On an outline map of Brazil, show with labels where you think each of the five photographs could have been taken. Give your map a title.

b Give reasons for your choices of location.

c Choose *three* photographs. Write down a more precise title for each of these photographs. Use your answers to **a** and **b** to help you.

⑧ Use your work from activities **4–7** to draft a paragraph to give a visitor to Brazil an introduction to the country.

Location, location, location

When geographers investigate a place, they often look first at its location. Location is usually described by linking the position of that place to the positions of other places. This is called the situation of the place. The starting point for your detailed investigation of Brazil is to ask the enquiry question:

Where is Brazil located?

All the maps on this page show Brazil.

🌀 Map **A** shows Brazil in its global situation.

🌀 Map **B** shows Brazil in its continental situation.

🌀 Map **C** shows São Paulo as a city within a region of Brazil.

The location of any place can be built up within a precise geographical **hierarchy**, like the one in diagram **D**.

B The situation of Brazil within the continent of South America

UK

Atlantic Ocean

Equator 0°

N

Brazil

Brasilia

0   3000 km

A Brazil in its global situation

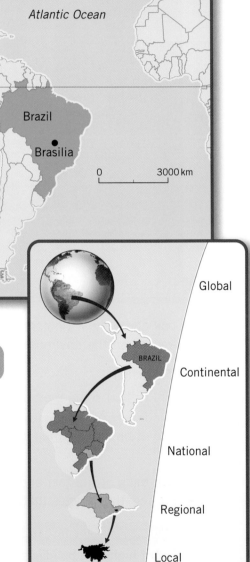

Global

BRAZIL

Continental

National

Regional

Local

D Building up a geographical hierarchy

Belo Horizonte

MINAS GERAIS

SÃO PAULO

Nova Iguaçu

São Paulo

Rio de Janeiro

Curitiba

Key
● Major cities

N

0   200   400 km

C The situation of São Paulo in its region

help!

Good geographers use terms like *north, south, east* and *west* to make their descriptions precise. Using latitude and longitude also helps to locate places exactly.

Activities

1 Use maps **A–B**, supported by your atlas, to locate Brazil within the world. Draw a simple sketch map and write two or three sentences to locate Brazil.

2 Draw a sketch map to show the situation of Brazil within the continent of South America. Write three sentences summarising what your sketch map shows about the country's situation.

3 Use your atlas to describe an air journey from the UK to Brasilia, the capital of Brazil.

🌀 Name the countries and oceans you pass over during your flight, as well as giving the direction you travel and the distances you cover.

🌀 The aircraft needs refuelling at an international airport every 2500 km. There are a number of ways you could do it – safe journey!

How big is Brazil?

If you look at maps **A** and **B**, you will not only see the situation of Brazil but also get a clear idea of the size or scale of the country. This gives a second aspect to the investigation, so you can ask a second enquiry question:

How big is Brazil?

The answer is more useful when the size is given in relation to the size of other countries.

Brazil is a very large country – it is the fifth largest in the world. You can see in table **C** how it compares with some other countries in South America.

A South America

B Europe

help!

Use the scale line on your map. Measure the distances using a ruler or by marking the edge of a piece of paper.

Country	Area
Argentina	2767
Bolivia	1099
Brazil	8512
Chile	757
Ecuador	272
Paraguay	407
Surinam	164
Uruguay	176
Venezuela	912

C The areas of some countries in South America (thousands of square kilometres)

Activities

① **a** Use a map of Brazil to measure the furthest distance from north to south across the country, and from east to west.

   b Now do the same for the UK. Write a sentence or two to compare the sizes of the countries.

   c Look at maps **A** and **B**. Work out approximately how many times the UK could fit into Brazil.

② Brazil is not the largest country in the world: Use an atlas to work out which countries are larger. Try to put them in order of size.

③ Table **C** only shows *some* of the countries in South America.

   a Estimate the size of the missing countries: French Guiana, Guyana, Colombia and Peru.

   b List all the countries in South America in order of size, starting with the largest.

What is Brazil like? What are the main differences within the country?

Case Study

Planning a trip to Brazil: can you get the contract?

Activity

1 You work for a company that is trying to plan a field trip to Brazil for school students. You need to convince the school that the students will be well informed about Brazil by the end of their three-week stay.

As you know by now, Brazil is a very large country. It is made up of several regions that have great differences. Some of these differences are shown in these six pages. You must make sure that, by the end of their trip, the students have a clear idea of what Brazil is like overall.

You have been asked to prepare and give a presentation showing the details of your field trip. This should include:

- A route map to show where the students will go and how long they will stay in each location

- The contrasts in the geography that the students will see in each part of the country that they visit

- The reasons for visiting the areas you propose

- The best time of the year for the visit, and any precautions that the students should take before starting this trip of a lifetime.

help!

Your presentation could include a display with photographs, itineraries, travel arrangements, timetables, short speeches, diagrams and maps. Useful websites for your research can be found at www.heinemann.co.uk/hotlinks (insert code 5171P). (ICT)

Briefing notes

Brazil is divided into five regions (see map **B**). These may help you plan your journey, but the students may not be able to visit all five in three weeks. The photographs, diagrams, maps and text on the following pages will give you some idea of each region's character.

What is the South and South-East of Brazil like?

This part of Brazil is divided into two – the South and South-East Regions. Temperatures in the region are tropical: 27–32°C in January, 16°C in July. It is never really uncomfortable by the coast as the sea breezes keep temperatures down, but it can be unpleasantly hot at night. In the South, temperatures are lower. Rainfall totals are high (over 1000 mm), and some areas do not have a dry season. The wettest season is during the summer months – November to April.

A High-rise buildings and factories in Belo Horizonte

B The regions of Brazil

N

0   1000 km

AMAZONIA

Amazon

Manaus •

Belém •

Fortaleza •

NORTH

Pôrto Velho •

Recife •

NORTH-EAST

RONDÔNIA

CENTRE-WEST

MATO GROSSO

Salvador •

Cuiabá •

Brasília

Belo Horizonte •

SOUTH-EAST

São Paulo •

Rio de Janeiro •

Curitiba •

SOUTH

Pôrto Alegre •

Fact file

Cities in the south-east of Brazil

- The cities contain the head offices of many international companies.
- The economy grew rapidly between 1960 and 1990 – an 'economic miracle'.
- Rapid growth has its costs, with high pollution levels and shortage of proper housing, clean water and rubbish disposal.

In the south-east of Brazil, the Brazilian highlands reach the coast to form an area of steep slopes. Development often only occurs on flat land. This region has the highest mountains of the country. The rest of Brazil is a land of flat horizons.

The south-east has always been important for Brazil. In 1850 the city of São Paulo began to grow because of the rich coffee estates nearby. Today, this is the main industrial region of Brazil. Most of the country's population is concentrated in this region around the three cities of São Paulo, Rio de Janeiro and Belo Horizonte. The area has an important steel industry. The blast furnaces use local iron ore and **charcoal** from the local forests. Agriculture is the most mechanised in the country. Large farms produce coffee, sugar cane and grains for **export**, as well as for food for the Brazilian people.

C Growing sugar cane is highly mechanised

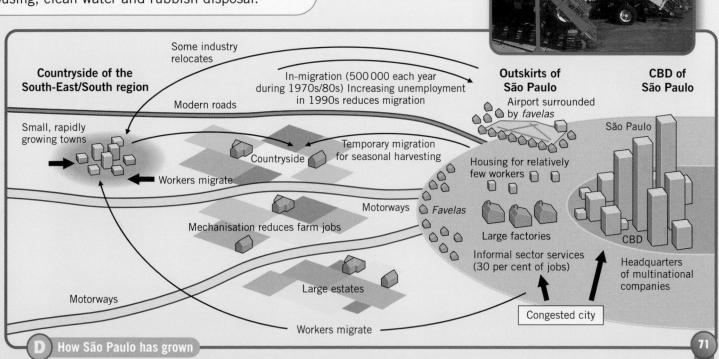

Countryside of the South-East/South region

Some industry relocates

In-migration (500 000 each year during 1970s/80s) Increasing unemployment in 1990s reduces migration

Outskirts of São Paulo

CBD of São Paulo

Modern roads

Airport surrounded by *favelas*

São Paulo

Small, rapidly growing towns

Countryside

Temporary migration for seasonal harvesting

Housing for relatively few workers

Workers migrate

Motorways

Favelas

Mechanisation reduces farm jobs

Large factories

CBD

Informal sector services (30 per cent of jobs)

Headquarters of multinational companies

Large estates

Motorways

Congested city

Workers migrate

D How São Paulo has grown

What is the Centre-West Region of Brazil like?

Inland from the crowded coast of the South-East Region are the high plains of the Mato Grosso. The mountains of the coastal area have merged into a vast **plateau** about 1000 metres high. The monotonous landscape can be seen in photograph **F**. Away from the coast, temperatures become higher and it is less **humid**. Annual rainfall is high (1700 mm) but there is a dry season from May to September. The natural vegetation of this area is **savanna** grassland.

E Cattle ranching in the Centre-West Region

Traditional life in the Centre-West Region

- Poor soils only allowed **extensive ranching** of cattle: fewer than one cow per hectare.

- The few mineral resources were quickly mined.

- Towns were few and far between. They were local market and services centres.

Changes to life in the Centre-West Region

- In 1960 a new capital city, Brasilia, was built.

- People migrated here as farming became more mechanised.

- Soya bean cultivation changed the farming landscape greatly during the late twentieth century.

F Brasilia

What is the North-East Region of Brazil like?

The north-east is much drier than the rest of Brazil, with less than 750 mm of rainfall. However, this rainfall is very unreliable. In the 1970s a terrible **drought** caused out-migration from this poor area. This was one cause of the dramatic growth in many Brazilizan cities, especially in the south-east.

The inland part of this region has the least rainfall. The São Francisco River flows through the area. The river often has great changes in water level, and its tributaries run dry during the dry season. In an attempt to supply water throughout the year, the river was dammed at Juàzeiro to form the Sobradinho Reservoir.

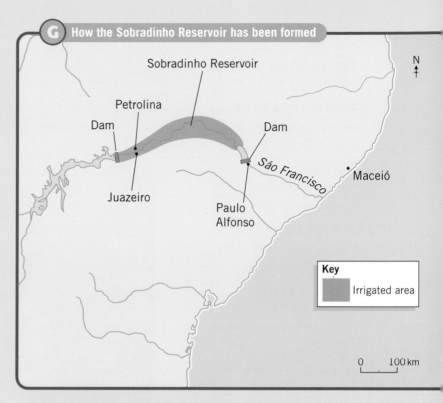

G How the Sobradinho Reservoir has been formed

Sobradinho Reservoir

Petrolina

Dam

Juazeiro

Paulo Alfonso

São Francisco

Dam

Maceió

N

Key
Irrigated area

0   100 km

Brazil invests in alcohol

Sugar cane can be processed to make ethanol (pure alcohol), which may be used as an alternative to petrol. The Brazilian government started a programme in the 1970s to increase ethanol production in the north-east. The aim was to help poor farmers in this underdeveloped area, as well as reducing the need to import oil. This idea may seem good, but sugar cane is grown on large farms, so valuable land is taken away from growing food.

Fact file

The North-East Region of Brazil

◎ It is the largest area of poverty in the Americas.

◎ Urban population is now greater than the rural population because of recent migration to cities.

◎ There is a high density of rural population.

◎ The standard of living is constantly threatened by a lack of basic needs, especially food.

H Farming in the north-east of Brazil

Disaster, famine, disease and drought ravage the land!

Starving mobs ransacked market stalls in a small town in the State of Pernambuco yesterday. A thousand people queued to fill their tins with drinking water. There have been lootings by hungry peasant farmers all over Ceara State. Ninety per cent of all crops have been destroyed by severe drought, which has followed three years of below-average rainfall.

Many people in the area farm very small plots and are unable to save money. Large-scale projects don't seem to make much difference to the plight of the poor.

The Brazilian government declared a state of emergency in the area last night.

I Newsflash from the North-East Region of Brazil, 24 January 1992

What is it like in the North Region?

An unending 'sea' of jungle full of exotic creatures

A landscape laden with moisture

Daily downpours of rain

Massive system that helps stabilise the global climate

Tall trees, both evergreen and broad-leaved

Contains one in thirty of the world's butterflies

Home to 2000 species of fish

One in five of the world's bird species live in one-fiftieth of the Earth's land surface

Hot and wet throughout the year, rotting even people's clothes

Full of stinging and biting creatures

Crawling with huge spiders, many with deadly bites

Home to tribal people who are threatened by 'western ways'

J Amazonia – the final frontier?

 idea Find out more at www.heinemann.co.uk/hotlinks (insert code 5171P)

In the north of Brazil the climate is **equatorial**, with rainfall totals of over 2000 mm. There is no dry season but some months are much wetter than others. The Amazon river flows through this region from west to east. Together with more than 1000 known tributaries, the Amazon makes up the largest river basin area in the world. The landscape is a huge lowland plain, but steep-sided river valleys cause local changes to the soil and vegetation. The Amazon in Brazil has a very gentle **gradient** throughout its 6400 kilometre course, with no land over 250 metres. Large boats can sail a long way up the Amazon, so it is an important transport route.

The **selvas** is the last large area of undeveloped tropical rainforest in the world. For many years the resources of the forest have been seen by the government as a great opportunity to increase the wealth of the country. For centuries people have farmed or gathered natural products like Brazil nuts, cocoa, indigo, vanilla oil and natural rubber from the rainforest. These activities were **sustainable** because they did no long-term damage to the forest environment. More recent developments have often been larger in scale and have had a much greater impact.

There are two main cities in this area: Manaus, the capital of the State of Amazonas, and Belém, which is near the mouth of the river. Both have grown very rapidly since 1990, partly because many of the large-scale agricultural development plans in this area have failed.

K How a rainforest works: an unending 'sea' of jungle full of exotic creatures

What is a developed country?

The students threw a party when they got home from their trip to Brazil. Several of them started talking about what a developed country was. It was a lively party and the discussion became quite heated ...

A developed country is simply a rich country! The rich countries of the world, places like UK or USA, are very developed.
Asma

Surely there is more to development than just money – hasn't happiness got something to do with being a developed person? A developed country is simply a country made up of mainly happy people.
Amy

Development is easy to measure. In developed countries, people on average have a high income. In poor, developing countries people on average have a low income.
Heidi

I'd say a developed country is one in which there is a good education system, a good medical system and a fair system of democratic government.
Kerrie

Whether a country is developed or not must include things like **sustainability** or inequality. I don't feel that Britain is a very developed country – we don't have a sustainable lifestyle. Since the 1980s the gap between the rich and the poor has been getting greater.
Su-yin

I think that the tribal people of the Amazon are among the most developed people in the world. They have lots of leisure time, even though life is short for most of them.
Joe

People are happy when they have money to do what they want – this means that they've probably got a good job which pays well. People in developed countries have got good jobs. Certainly most of them aren't sweating in the fields trying to farm on poor soils with little machinery to help.
Carl

How can a country get developed if it is in debt? No country can be developed if it imports more than it exports.
Brett

Developed countries have met the basic needs of all their people, like having enough food, access to water and proper housing.
Jasbir

Activities

1 Read the views of the nine people on the opposite page.

   a Select the person that you agree with most and give a reason for your decision.

   b Repeat the activity for the person you disagree with most.

2 Jasbir gave some examples of basic human needs. What other human needs would you have added to this list?

3 Some people have a rather narrow view of what a country's development is about. Other people feel that the definition is based upon a large number of factors. Divide the views of the nine people into two columns based upon whether you think they have a narrow or broad view of development. The table has been started for you.

Broad view of development	Narrow view of development
Amy	

4 Use a full page to produce a brainstorm diagram showing all the factors that could be used to define development. Use all the views of the people involved in the discussion as well as some of your own ideas.

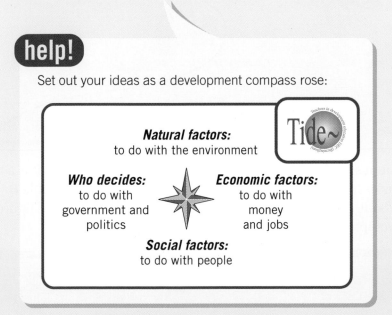

help!

Set out your ideas as a development compass rose:

Natural factors:
to do with the environment

Tide~

Who decides:
to do with
government and
politics

Economic factors:
to do with
money
and jobs

Social factors:
to do with people

5 Now it is time to come to a conclusion:

   What is a developed country?

   Imagine you were at the party. Write down what you would have said after hearing all nine opinions. Try to end up with the best definition of what you think 'a developed country' is.

6 **a** Add your definition to your geography word bank.

   b Look back through pages 64–75 and add any other key words you need to remember.

How developed is Brazil?

There are a number of ways to look at how developed a country is.
One way is to use a map like **A**, which shows world development based
upon Gross National Product.

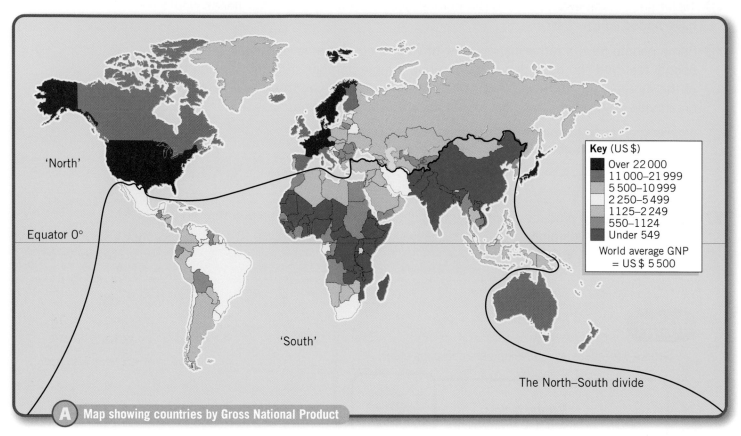

Key (US $)
- Over 22 000
- 11 000–21 999
- 5 500–10 999
- 2 250–5 499
- 1 125–2 249
- 550–1 124
- Under 549

World average GNP
= US $ 5 500

'North'

Equator 0°

'South'

The North–South divide

A Map showing countries by Gross National Product

Although this way of looking at development seems straightforward, many geographers think it is a bit
too simple. **Economic development** is easier to measure than other forms of development. Table **B**
shows some different information for six South American countries and the UK. Some of these figures
may be more important for assessing development than others.

Country	GNP (US $)	Safe water (%)	Adult literacy rate (%)	Life expectancy (years)	IMR (per thousand)	Population growth (%)	Energy consumption (kg oil equivalent)
Argentina	11 728	65	97	73	19	1.4	1 730
Bolivia	2 205	55	87	62	60	2.2	548
Brazil	6 460	72	85	67	33	1.7	1 051
Chile	8 507	85	95	75	10	1.6	1 574
Guyana	760	83	98	64	57	0.8	426
Venezuela	5 706	79	94	73	21	2.4	2 526
UK	20 314	100	99	77	6	0.3	3 863

Data taken from 1980 –1998

B Development indicators

Getting Technical ▼

- **Gross National Product (GNP)** – the wealth a country produces, divided by the total population. GNP is measured in US dollars.
- **Safe water** – percentage of people who have access to clean water.
- **Adult literacy rate** – percentage of adults who can read and write.
- **Life expectancy** – the average number of years people can expect to live.
- **Infant mortality rate (IMR)** – the number of babies who die before their first birthday, out of every thousand born.
- **Population growth** – how fast the population is growing, in percentage each year.
- **Energy consumption** – the average energy each person in a country uses, measured in kilograms of oil equivalent.

Activities

1 Use map **A** to put these countries in order of economic development. Start with the most developed country.

Brazil Argentina Bolivia Chile Guyana Venezuela UK

2 Write a paragraph describing the general pattern of world economic development as shown in map **A**.

3 a Look at the development data for seven countries in table **B**. Choose the four indicators which you think give the best overall picture of development. Explain why you have chosen them.

b For each of your four chosen indicators, rank the seven countries in order of development.

c Draw up a final league table based upon the overall average ranks. Highlight the position of Brazil within your league table.

4 In a group, produce a display that compares the development of the seven countries shown in table **B**.

5 **Extension**

Use the Internet to research further figures to make your comparison fairer. You could start by going to www.heinemann.co.uk/hotlinks (insert code 5171P) and looking at schools on the website listed. ICT

help!

You could use a writing frame to help you extend your description.

> The most economically developed continents in the world are …
>
> Countries in these continents have GNPs of about …
>
> The least economically developed continents in the world are …
>
> The other continents include …

help!

In your group display, you could include:

- a map showing the location of all the countries
- very brief summaries about each country
- your four league tables – find a way of showing these graphically and put them around your map. Add the final league table.

6 Write a short paragraph comparing Brazil's development with that of one other country in your league table.

7 Explain how cartoon **C** shows the difficulties facing less developed countries.

C

> The furniture and banana tree come to $6.27 – that means you still owe, er … $999,999,993.73

US BANKS REPOSSESSIONS Co (SOUTH AMERICA)

How successful has development been in Brazil?

A number of developments that have recently occurred in Brazil are discussed in the next five pages. The activities for this section are on page 85. You may be asked to investigate the enquiry question above in groups.

The recent history of Brazil has been full of plans to try to develop the rich resources of the country in order to improve the lives of the Brazilian people. Many of these developments focused on the final frontier – Amazonia.

Transport developments

To make the centre and north of Brazil richer, the government has a vast road-building programme. The dream of the Brazilian government is to build roads westwards until there is a link right across the continent from the Atlantic to the Pacific Ocean. The three main **arterial roads** are:

- the Trans-Amazonian Highway, built in the 1970s

- the Brazilian Road (BR364), which opened up the jungle states of Rondonia and Acre in the mid 1980s

- the Northern Perimetral Highway, which is still under construction.

Feeder roads branch off the main roads to allow farming and settlement of the land. Many roads in Amazonia become impassable in the wet season because they have no proper surface. Paving the roads is very costly and the government has to borrow money to do it.

Roads are one of the main ways to open up the forest. They allow migrants, services and food to be brought into the forest and timber, minerals and farm products to be brought out – building roads is the first stage in destroying the forest.

A The Brazilian Road (BR364) cuts through the rainforest in Amazonia

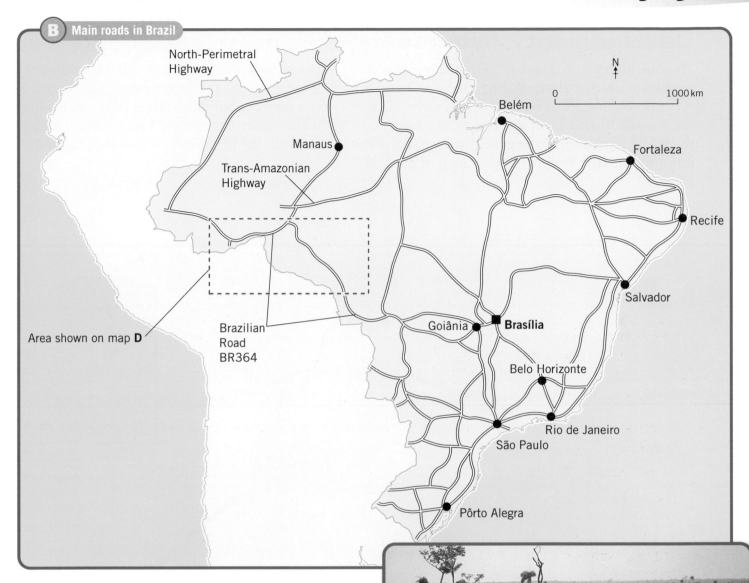

B Main roads in Brazil

North-Perimetral Highway

Belém

Fortaleza

Manaus

Trans-Amazonian Highway

Recife

Area shown on map **D**

Brazilian Road BR364

Goiânia

Brasília

Salvador

Belo Horizonte

Rio de Janeiro

São Paulo

Pôrto Alegra

0   1000 km

N

C During and after the destruction of the rainforest

Cattle ranching

Cattle ranching has become one of the main reasons why the rainforest has been destroyed in Amazonia. The ranches are usually very large and many are owned by large, powerful meat-producing companies. The trees are cut down to make room for cattle pasture. There is a great demand for beef in the 'hamburger' culture of the USA, Japan and Europe, and Brazil exports much of the beef it produces. Cattle ranching does provide employment, but one cowboy can manage over 3000 cattle. Unfortunately Amazonia's poor soils do not support good grass growth, so weeds grow which can only be eradicated by **herbicides**. As a result, the land eventually becomes useless. The ranchers abandon the land and wait for land prices to rise before making a massive profit. As more roads are built, more forest timber becomes accessible and more minerals are discovered, so most people expect that land prices will go up.

Developments in Rondônia

The Brazilian government encouraged massive migration into Rondônia during the 1980s to try to give poorer farmers some land of their own. First the Porto Velho road (BR364) had to be paved, and the World Bank loaned the government much of the money to do this. Unfortunately much of the land which used to support lush tropical rainforest became useless for farming after a few years. Many new settlers abandoned their land and headed further on into the jungle to see if they had better luck with the next piece of land they cleared.

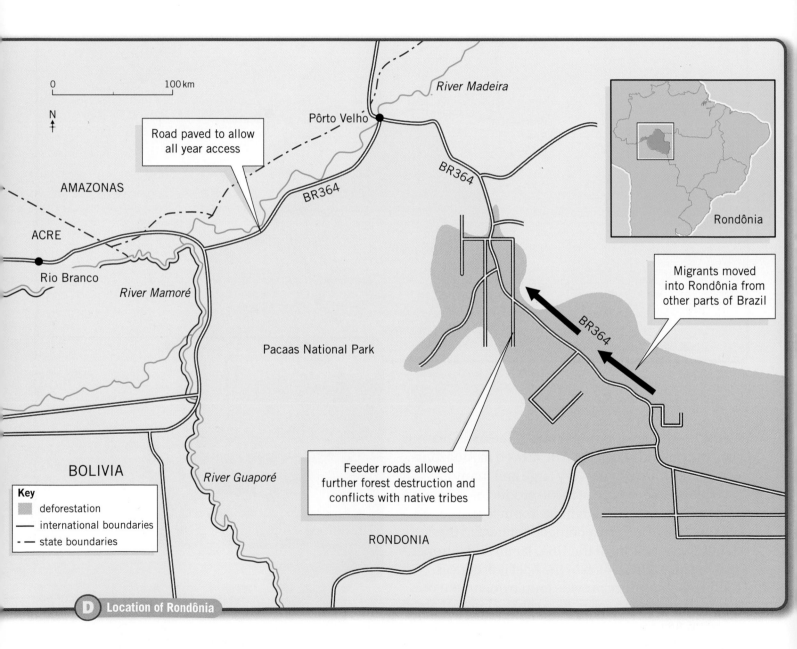

0 — 100 km

N

River Madeira

Pôrto Velho

Road paved to allow all year access

AMAZONAS

BR364

ACRE

Rio Branco

River Mamoré

BR364

Rondônia

Migrants moved into Rondônia from other parts of Brazil

BR364

Pacaas National Park

BOLIVIA

Key
- deforestation
- international boundaries
- state boundaries

River Guaporé

Feeder roads allowed further forest destruction and conflicts with native tribes

RONDONIA

D Location of Rondônia

E Rainforest destruction in Rondônia – the area shown is 240 km²

Key

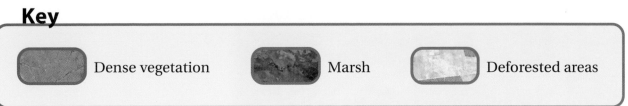

Dense vegetation   Marsh   Deforested areas

Mining in the Amazon jungle

The Amazon has great mineral wealth. One of the largest mining projects is in the Carajás mountains. One of the largest known deposits of iron ore in the world is here. The ore is very pure, containing 66 per cent iron. Since 1980 the Brazilian government has opened up the area. As a result, 100 square kilometres of rainforest have been destroyed. A 900 km railway line to a deep-water port at São Luis has been built to export the iron ore.

The project uses power **generated** by the nearby Tucurui **Hydro power plant**. Building this meant that another 2000 square kilometres of forest was destroyed. Nearby forest is also under pressure for making charcoal, which is needed to produce the iron. The company that developed the area has now agreed to protect 12 000 square kilometres of land and the native people who live there. In exchange, it wants to mine a further 4120 square kilometres. Many environmentalists ask whether twenty years' supply of iron ore is worth the ecological damage.

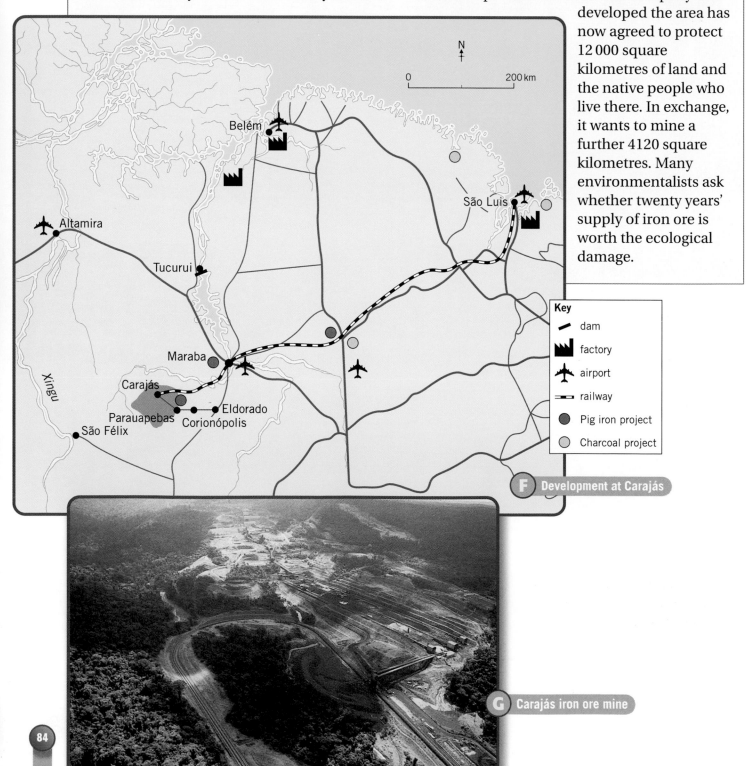

Key

∖	dam
🏭	factory
✈	airport
–∎–	railway
●	Pig iron project
●	Charcoal project

F Development at Carajás

G Carajás iron ore mine

How is Brazil changing and what are the impacts of these changes?

Don't re-read every single sentence! Try to skim read and look out for dates quoted in the text.

Activities

① Draw a timeline to record the important events in Brazil's attempts to develop the country since 1960. You will need to look back over earlier pages of this unit. Set your timeline out like this. Remember to allow lots of space – if things start to get cluttered, use a key.

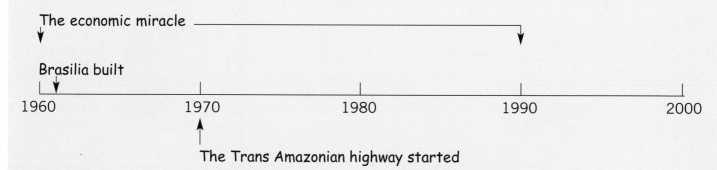

② Choose a colour for each of the regions you studied earlier in the unit and make a key. For each change that you have marked on your diagram, shade neatly behind the writing to show which part of Brazil was affected.

③ Write a short paragraph to summarise what your timeline diagram shows about the developments that have occurred in Brazil since 1960.

④ Choose three of the changes that you have marked on your diagram. Try to assess how successful each of the developments has been. Set your work out like this.

Development: Sobradinho Reservoir	Region: NE Brazil
Brief description of development:	
Good things about the change:	
Bad things about the change:	
Verdict:	

⑤ Work out a league table for the developments that you have considered in activity **4**. Put the most successful development first. Write a short summary to describe any pattern that your league table shows.

Review and reflect

Looking at the lives of six Brazilians

My name is Renato and I've had a varied life. My family started off in the south of Brazil, in the State of Parana. We had no land. Then big machinery was brought into the large estate farms and took away the jobs of casual workers. We headed out to Rondônia twenty years ago. I dreamed of owning my own bit of land, but things didn't work out. Here we are in Porto Velho. My son has a small café in the town and I help out when my health allows me. I've never really got used to the climate.

They call me Yano. Things have changed for us over the last twenty years. We have to fight to keep our lands where we used to make a living. We can't catch as many fish as we used to. We can now trade forest products but there is so much pressure to change the forest that our old way of life will soon be a memory.

I'm called Maria. Life has always been difficult here in north-east Brazil. My grandparents farmed in the fertile valley of the São Francisco river. That was before the dam was constructed. I suppose our country needs the electricity. They resettled our family but the land we got wasn't as good. I'm not sure that I can face farming as my parents did.

Map A

- 0 — 1000 km
- N
- Manaus
- Belém
- NORTH
- NORTH-EAST
- Rondônia
- CENTRE-WEST
- Mato Grosso
- **Brasília**
- Belo Horizonte
- SOUTH-EAST
- São Paulo
- Rio de Janeiro
- Curitiba
- SOUTH

A

I'm Luiz Boaz and I work as a beef exporter, so I need to be near our headquarters in São Paulo. I live in one of the city centre apartments but am often away on business. Our lifestyle is good – like many other Brazilians, we can afford a live-in maid. Our children go to good schools.

Everyone knows me in my factory; they called me B.A. I suppose I am lucky to have this job. The working conditions are good and everyone is friendly. Pepsi built this factory out in the small provincial town of Jundiai, not too far from São Paulo. Brazil is a great country to live in.

My name is Somália da Silva. I live on the outskirts of Rio de Janeiro in a *favela* called Vigário Geral. It is a tough place in Rio's North Zone. I have six daughters and am pregnant again. We all stay in the room furthest from the street during the night for fear of stray bullets and police raids on the *favela*.

You need to be familiar with all the investigations that you have done on Brazil as you work through these activities. The sections on the regions of Brazil and the developments are especially important. The activities are best done in groups of up to six people.

Activities

1 Read the statements made by the six people on the opposite page. Spend some time within your group deciding who is going to represent each of the six characters. Write down the results of your discussion.

2 For each character that you represent, write a full description of the kind of life they lead.

help!

Start off by using what the character has said on page 86, then think about the following topics which have run through this unit:

- the **location** of where they live within Brazil

- the **natural** environment there, e.g. climate, vegetation and relief

- the **economy** of the area, e.g. the sort of jobs people do

- the **social** geography of the area, e.g. family life, population density, birth and death rate, life expectancy

- the **changes** that are occurring in the area.

3 Copy the table below. Work out a **conflict matrix** for each of the characters:

Somália	Renato	B.A.	Luiz	Maria	Yano
Somália					
	Renato			✓	
		B.A.			
			Luiz		
				Maria	
					Yano

- If you think the two characters would share many of the same interests and agree with each other about how Brazil was being developed, mark with a tick (✓). One has been done for you.

- If you think they would disagree, mark with a cross (✗).

- If you think they would have no strong feeling mark with a wavy line (‿‿).

- Put two ticks (✓✓) or two crosses (✗✗) if the agreement or disagreement is very great.

4 Give reasons for the decisions you have made in activity **3**. Focus in particular on the character or characters you represent.

5
Extension

Work out a new conflict matrix for how you think things might change over the next ten years. Remember to justify your decisions.

6 Limestone landscapes of England

A Stalactites in a limestone cave

B Limestone quarry

C Limestone scar

D This cathedral is built of limestone

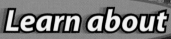

Learn about

Limestone is a unique rock that creates some spectacular landforms. Some of the best examples are found in the Yorkshire Dales National Park. Limestone is under threat from economic activities which take place in the landscape, such as farming, quarrying and tourism. These landscapes are protected by conservation orders to make sure that they survive into the future. In this unit you will learn:

- what different types of rocks can be found in upland areas in England

- what is special about areas of limestone

- how limestone was formed and what features are typical of limestone areas

- what is distinctive about the Yorkshire Dales

- where the water goes in a limestone area, and what it looks like underground

- how the limestone landscape is being changed.

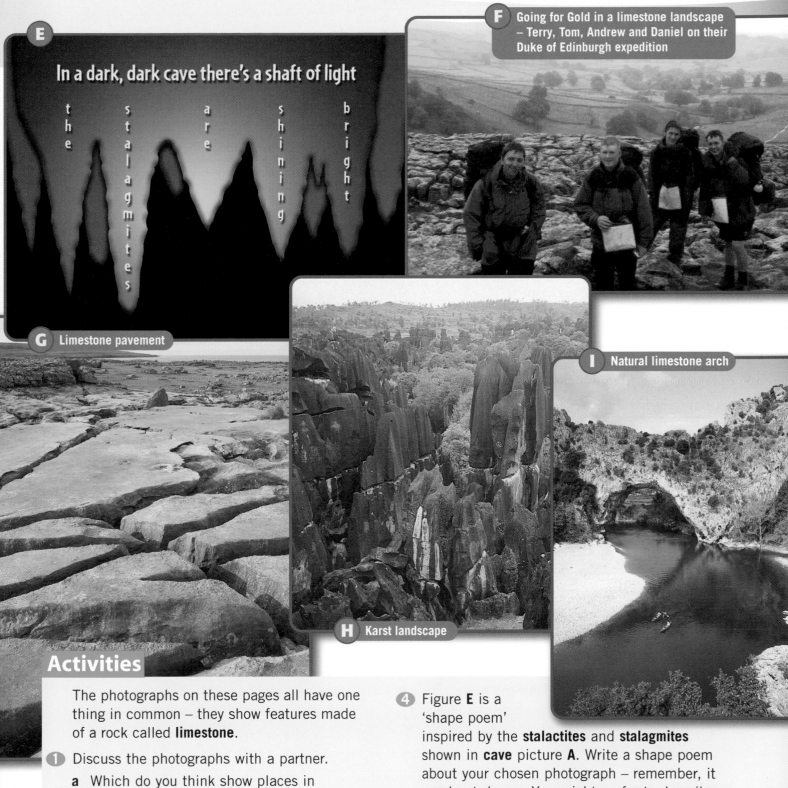

E

In a dark, dark cave there's a shaft of light

the stalagmites are shining bright

F Going for Gold in a limestone landscape – Terry, Tom, Andrew and Daniel on their Duke of Edinburgh expedition

G Limestone pavement

I Natural limestone arch

H Karst landscape

Activities

The photographs on these pages all have one thing in common – they show features made of a rock called **limestone**.

1 Discuss the photographs with a partner.

a Which do you think show places in England?

b Which show places in other countries?

c What do you think are the key features of limestone?

2 List all the ways that limestone is being used by the people in the photographs. What other uses do you think limestone has?

3 Choose the photograph that you like best. Explain to your partner why you like it.

4 Figure **E** is a 'shape poem' inspired by the **stalactites** and **stalagmites** shown in **cave** picture A. Write a shape poem about your chosen photograph – remember, it need not rhyme. You might prefer to describe the things that you see as a story instead. 📖

5 Begin a word bank of words about limestone. Start with the words in **bold** on these pages. Use the glossary on page 142 to check their meanings. Add more words as you work through the unit. 📖

England rocks!

England has a huge variety of landscapes. In this unit you are going to discover some of the most beautiful scenery in this country and find out about limestone landscapes. England has some flat land (**lowland** areas) and also some hills and mountains (**upland** areas).

Look carefully at map **A**, which is a relief map of England and Wales. Relief maps show the landscape of a place. The map is shaded using a series of colours to show the highest and lowest land. This is called **layer shading**. The highest land on map **A** is shaded in brown and the lowest land in green.

A relief map also shows the names of the hills and mountain ranges. Sometimes the highest points have a number beside them to show how high that point is above sea level. The biggest rivers are named and coloured in blue, and so are the lakes and seas.

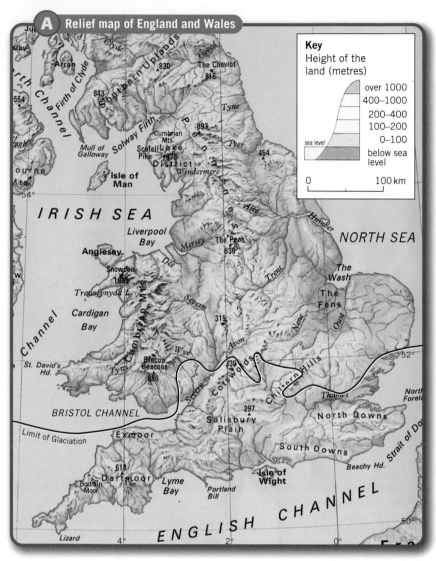

A Relief map of England and Wales

Key
Height of the land (metres)

over 1000
400–1000
200–400
100–200
0–100
below sea level
sea level

0   100 km

Activities

1. Look at relief map **A**. Find the place where you live. Use the layer shading to work out how high it is in metres above sea level.

2. Look at the list of statements below. Decide if each one is true or false. Then write down the true statements to describe the landscapes of England.

   a There is no land above 300 metres in England.

   b The south of England is more hilly than the north.

   c All low-lying land, below 100 metres, is in the east.

   d The highest mountain in England is called Scafell Pike.

   e The highest peak is 619 metres above sea level.

   f Most of the upland areas are in the north of England.

3. Now add two more sentences of your own to finish your paragraph about the landscapes of England. Use an atlas to name some places that are in upland and lowland areas.

Rock types

There are many rock types in England. The geological timescale **B** shows the length of time over which rocks were formed. England's oldest rocks were formed more than 600 million years ago during the Pre-Cambrian period. Dinosaurs roamed the Earth during the Jurassic period, only 180 million years ago. In general, the oldest rocks are the hardest (most resistant to erosion).

Limestone is a **sedimentary rock**. There are two types of limestone in England:

- Oolitic (Jurassic) limestone (135–180 million years old)
- Carboniferous limestone (225– 600 million years old).

The landscapes in this unit are typical of Carboniferous limestone.

Activities

4 Compare relief map **A** with map **C** showing the rock types of England.

   a What do you notice about the pattern of rock types?

   b Which rock types are found in upland areas? Which types are found in the lowlands?

5 **a** Make a copy of the geological timescale **B**.

   b Label sedimentary, **igneous** and **metamorphic** rocks against the correct period on the scale: 'Getting Technical' will tell you how old these rock types are. Use different colours for your labels.

   c Label Jurassic and Carboniferous limestone on your scale.

Getting Technical ▼

Sedimentary rocks are made of bits of rock (sediments) which were laid down in layers, usually under water. Over a very long time the sediments are squeezed (compressed) into new rocks (0–600 million years).

Igneous rocks were formed when molten rock (**magma**) from deep inside the Earth interior cooled down to form rocks (290–600 million years).

Metamorphic rocks are sedimentary or igneous rocks which have been changed by heat or pressure (over 500 million years).

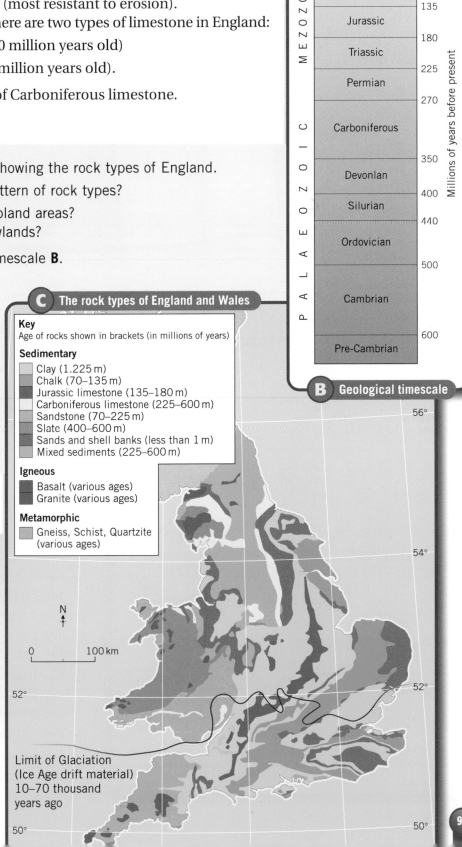

C The rock types of England and Wales

Key
Age of rocks shown in brackets (in millions of years)

Sedimentary
- Clay (1.225 m)
- Chalk (70–135 m)
- Jurassic limestone (135–180 m)
- Carboniferous limestone (225–600 m)
- Sandstone (70–225 m)
- Slate (400–600 m)
- Sands and shell banks (less than 1 m)
- Mixed sediments (225–600 m)

Igneous
- Basalt (various ages)
- Granite (various ages)

Metamorphic
- Gneiss, Schist, Quartzite (various ages)

Limit of Glaciation (Ice Age drift material) 10–70 thousand years ago

B Geological timescale

CAINOZOIC	Pleistocene	
	Pliocene	1.0
	Miocene	11
	Oligocene	25
	Eocene	40
	Palaeocene	60
		70
MEZOZOIC	Cretaceous	135
	Jurassic	180
	Triassic	225
	Permian	270
PALAEOZOIC	Carboniferous	350
	Devonlan	400
	Silurian	440
	Ordovician	500
	Cambrian	600
	Pre-Cambrian	

Millions of years before present

Why is limestone so special?

A LONG, LONG TIME AGO...

...EVEN BEFORE THE DINOSAURS

England was covered by a shallow tropical sea – a bit like where the Great Barrier Reef is forming today.

As the small animals and corals that lived in the sea died, their shells and skeletons fell to the bottom.

A thick layer built up over millions of years. As it squashed and hardened, it eventually turned into limestone.

A

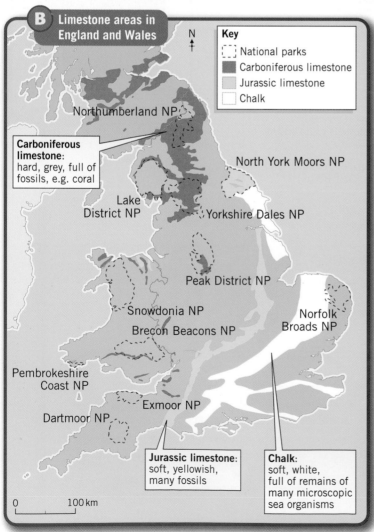

B Limestone areas in England and Wales

N

Key
- National parks
- Carboniferous limestone
- Jurassic limestone
- Chalk

Northumberland NP

Carboniferous limestone: hard, grey, full of fossils, e.g. coral

North York Moors NP

Lake District NP

Yorkshire Dales NP

Peak District NP

Snowdonia NP

Norfolk Broads NP

Brecon Beacons NP

Pembrokeshire Coast NP

Exmoor NP

Dartmoor NP

Jurassic limestone: soft, yellowish, many fossils

Chalk: soft, white, full of remains of many microscopic sea organisms

0   100 km

Carboniferous limestone is one of the oldest rocks in the British Isles. There are many places where it can be found – the largest areas are in the north of England and the Republic of Ireland.

Cartoon **A** shows how limestone was formed. Between 270 and 325 million years ago, northern England was an ocean bed near the Equator. Because these warm tropical seas were rich in sea creatures, you will find many fossils in these rocks.

Limestone is formed from sediments which collected at the bottom of the warm seas and the remains of the sea creatures. Carboniferous limestone is made of **calcium carbonate**. The calcium came from the shells of the sea creatures and the carbon from the softer body parts.

Map **B** shows the three sedimentary rocks in England and Wales that are made from sea creatures: chalk, Jurassic limestone and Carboniferous limestone.

- Chalk and Jurassic limestone can hold water – they have tiny holes in them and are **porous**.

- Carboniferous limestone is special because it is permeable – water can disappear underground and flow right through it!

Limestone's special: rock structure

Carboniferous limestone rock creates unique scenery because of its special structure. It was laid down in layers; as it solidified and was moved by earth movements it cracked into large blocks. If you sliced through the limestone, it would look a bit like a brick wall. The spaces between the 'bricks' are called **joints**. They let water pass along them, so when it rains the rainwater travels down through the rock until it can go no further. Eventually some comes back out to the surface as a **spring**. The special structure of limestone is shown on diagram **C**.

D The cracks in this rock are called joints

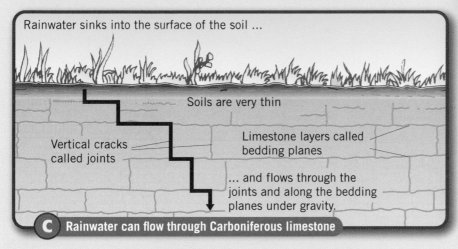

Rainwater sinks into the surface of the soil ...

Soils are very thin

Vertical cracks called joints

Limestone layers called bedding planes

... and flows through the joints and along the bedding planes under gravity.

C Rainwater can flow through Carboniferous limestone

E This limestone statue has been weathered by rainwater

Limestone's special: destruction by water

In the past few million years there have been several **ice ages** when the climate got much colder – huge ice sheets covered the land surface. When the climate got warmer again, the meltwater carved out valleys and dumped mud and boulders.

Much of England's Carboniferous limestone scenery was shaped by ice or meltwater. Since then, the rainy weather in England has helped to shape the rocks by the process of *weathering* (look back at page 19).

The weather – wind, rain, heat and cold – affects rocks where they are exposed to it, and they break down into smaller pieces. Rainwater is a weak acid. Calcium carbonate, which makes up limestone, is alkaline. The acidic water reacts with the alkaline rock and the chemical reaction dissolves the limestone. This is an example of *chemical weathering*.

Activities

1. Look at photo **E**. Describe what the statue looks like now compared with when it was new. Explain how the changes have occurred and suggest what might happen in the future.

2. Use the information on these two pages to produce a poster about limestone. It should include facts about the rock, an explanation of how limestone is weathered and a map to show where you might go to see limestone in England. You could use an ICT package to present your information. (ICT)

F The chemical reaction between rainwater and limestone

$$CaCO_3 + H_2O + CO_2 = Ca(HCO_3)_2$$

calcium carbonate + water + carbon dioxide = calcium bicarbonate (soluble)

What are typical limestone features?

Limestone is a rock that produces unique scenery because of its special structure and properties – it is permeable and is dissolved by rainwater. These two properties lead to the creation of landforms like **swallow holes**, **limestone pavements**, **caves** and **caverns**, and **limestone scars**.

You can see typical limestone features in diagram **A** and read about them in the boxes on pages 94–96.

Sinks and swallow holes

Rivers which flow across the landscape disappear underground when they reach an area of limestone. Some rivers seem to disappear as the water sinks into the limestone – this is called a **sink**. In other cases the water flows down a large hole into a cavern below. This is called a **swallow hole**. Photograph **B** shows one of the most famous swallow holes in England – Gaping Gill in Yorkshire. Here the river, Fell Beck, falls 110 metres into a cavern the size of a cathedral!

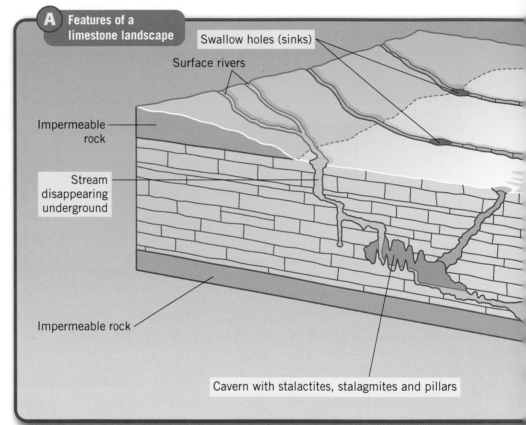

A Features of a limestone landscape

Swallow holes (sinks)

Surface rivers

Impermeable rock

Stream disappearing underground

Impermeable rock

Cavern with stalactites, stalagmites and pillars

B The swallow hole at Gaping Gill

The river reappears!

When the underground river reaches a layer of rock that it cannot flow through, it flows over it until it reaches the surface again at a **resurgence** or **spring**. This can be seen very clearly in **C** at the bottom of Malham Cove, a limestone scar in Yorkshire.

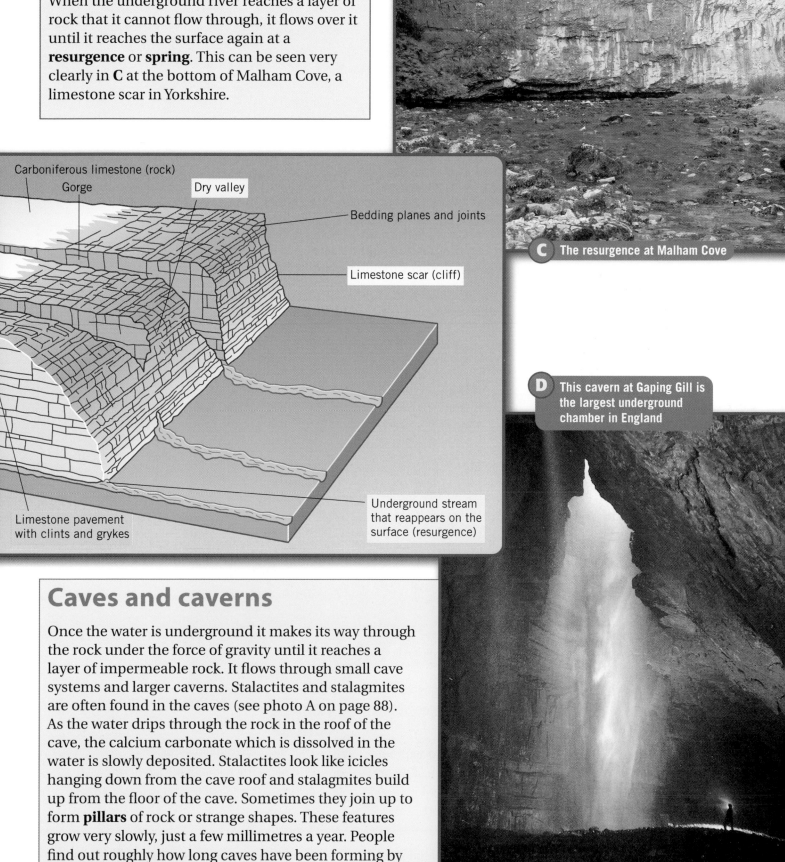

C The resurgence at Malham Cove

Carboniferous limestone (rock)

Gorge

Dry valley

Bedding planes and joints

Limestone scar (cliff)

Limestone pavement with clints and grykes

Underground stream that reappears on the surface (resurgence)

D This cavern at Gaping Gill is the largest underground chamber in England

Caves and caverns

Once the water is underground it makes its way through the rock under the force of gravity until it reaches a layer of impermeable rock. It flows through small cave systems and larger caverns. Stalactites and stalagmites are often found in the caves (see photo A on page 88). As the water drips through the rock in the roof of the cave, the calcium carbonate which is dissolved in the water is slowly deposited. Stalactites look like icicles hanging down from the cave roof and stalagmites build up from the floor of the cave. Sometimes they join up to form **pillars** of rock or strange shapes. These features grow very slowly, just a few millimetres a year. People find out roughly how long caves have been forming by measuring stalactites and stalagmites.

Dry valleys

During the Ice Age, the water was not able to flow through the limestone because it was frozen. But when the ice melted, the water on the surface of the land carved wide valleys. Today these valleys do not have any rivers. Why? Because the water sinks into the limestone and flows underground. These features are called **dry valleys**.

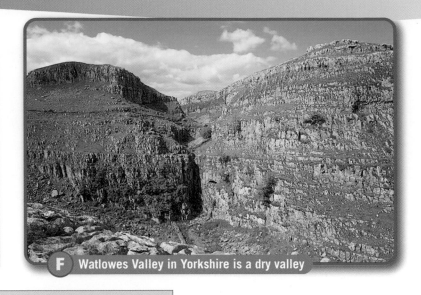

F Watlowes Valley in Yorkshire is a dry valley

Limestone pavements

When rock is exposed at the surface, the blocks of limestone can be clearly seen. This feature is called a **limestone pavement**. The flat blocks of rock are called **clints** and the gaps between them, which have been enlarged by weathering, are called **grykes**.

Limestone scars

Most limestone uplands have areas where the rock is exposed. These vertical rock faces are called **scars**. They can be many hundreds of metres high and are often used by rock climbers.

G A limestone pavement in Yorkshire

H Gordale Scar in the Yorkshire Dales

Activities

1. Use the information on these three pages to explain what each landform is in your geography word bank.

2. In groups, decide upon one landform to explain in detail. Produce a fact card about your chosen feature. Make sure that your work is well presented so that it could form part of a limestone display.

3. Present your work to the class. One person could be the 'expert' in the 'hot seat' and the rest of the group could ask them questions.

help!

Your fact card should include:
- *What* is the name of the landform?
- *Where* is it found in a limestone area?
- *How* is it formed?
- *Why* is it only found in a limestone area?
- *Name* some examples. You could use other textbooks, the Internet or an encyclopaedia.

What is the limestone like in the Yorkshire Dales?

Case Study

The Yorkshire Dales has one of the largest areas of limestone in England. It is one of eleven protected areas called **National Parks**. A National Park receives special care which helps people to enjoy them now and to protect them for the future.

About 19 000 people live in the Yorkshire Dales National Park, and the land is mostly owned by farmers. Each year over eight million people come to visit the National Park to view the spectacular scenery, many from the nearby cities of northern England.

A National Parks in northern England

0   100 km

N

Key
- National Park
- City

Northumberland NP
Yorkshire Dales NP
Newcastle-upon-Tyne
North York Moors NP
Lake District NP
Peak District NP
Leeds
Liverpool
Sheffield
Manchester

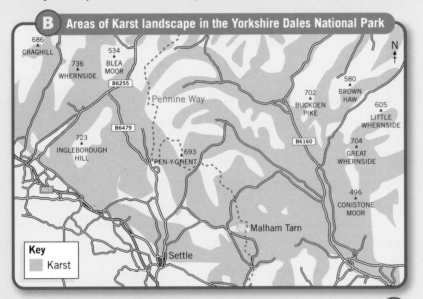

B Areas of Karst landscape in the Yorkshire Dales National Park

686 CRAGHILL
534 BLEA MOOR
736 WHERNSIDE
B6255
Pennine Way
580 BROWN HAW
702 BUCKDEN PIKE
605 LITTLE WHERNSIDE
B6479
723 INGLEBOROUGH HILL
693 PEN-Y-GHENT
B6160
704 GREAT WHERNSIDE
A65
496 CONISTONE MOOR
Malham Tarn
Settle

N

Key
- Karst

The Yorkshire Dales National Park is a popular area to visit for day trips, short breaks or longer holidays. Postcard **C** shows some of the most attractive areas and two of the region's three highest peaks: Pen-y-Ghent (694 m) and Great Whernside (704 m). From these hills you get marvellous views of the surrounding limestone areas.

C

Pen-y-Ghent

Whernside

The Settle viaduct in Ribblesdale

Malham village

Activity

1. Look at the information on pages 97–103 about the Yorkshire Dales National Park.

   a Design a leaflet about the National Park and its scenery for visitors to pick up at the Tourist Information Centres. The leaflet should be on one side of A4. You could use a publishing or drawing package on a computer to design it. ICT

   b Add some extra research from the Internet. You could use the website at www.heinemann.co.uk/hotlinks (insert code 5171P) or use a search engine to find Yorkshire Dales information.

Rocks and rain in Yorkshire

The Ingleborough area is one of the most famous limestone areas in Yorkshire, England. Photograph **F** on page 99 shows Ingleborough Hill, and the maps and diagrams on these pages show the area in lots of other ways.

Map **D** is a 1:50 000 Ordnance Survey map of the area. It shows Ingleborough Hill and Simon Fell, and the footpath from the summit to the swallow hole, Gaping Gill. The OS map **G** shows more detail because it has a scale of 1:25 000, so it is twice as big as **A**. Hikers use this type of map because it shows the landscape in more detail.

Both maps have **contour lines**, drawn in brown, which join places of equal height and show how steep the land is. A cross-section diagram can be used to look more closely at the shape of the land. Drawing a cross-section is like taking a slice through the land to see what it is like in reality.

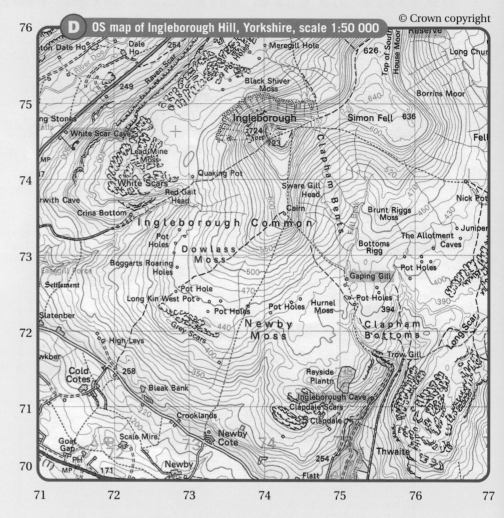

D OS map of Ingleborough Hill, Yorkshire, scale 1:50 000

© Crown copyright

Cross-section **E** has been drawn along a line from A to B on map **G**. It shows the route down from the summit of Ingleborough Hill, via Gaping Gill to Beck Head.

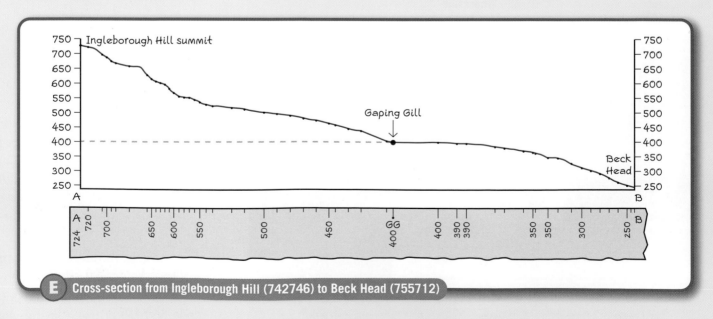

E Cross-section from Ingleborough Hill (742746) to Beck Head (755712)

When it rains, the water can flow across the surface of the rock at the top of Ingleborough Hill because it is made of **millstone grit**. This is an impermeable rock, so water cannot pass through it and streams like Fell Beck can flow on top of it. When Fell Beck meets limestone rock it disappears underground down Gaping Gill, a swallow hole. The water then flows underground and reappears at Beck Head, which is point B on the cross-section.

F Ingleborough Hill

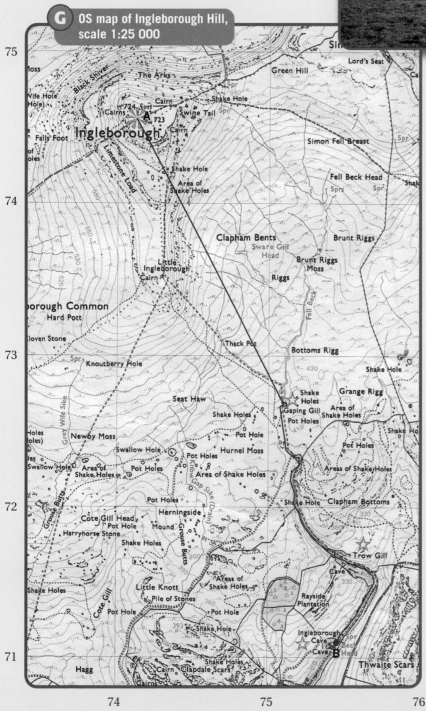

G OS map of Ingleborough Hill, scale 1:25 000

© Crown copyright

Getting Technical

◉ Contour lines join places of the same height at 10 metre intervals.

The closer together the contour lines are, the steeper the land.

240
230
220
210
200

120
110
100

◉ Hills are shown as contour rings.

Activities

2 Draw your own copy of the cross-section from the summit of Ingleborough Hill to Beck Head. If you need help, look back at the How to ... box on page 9.

3 Add the dotted line to show where the impermeable rock ends and the limestone begins at Gaping Gill.

4 Add the river to your cross-section, using a blue line to show where the water goes underground and then reappears at Beck Head.

5 Add labels or write a short paragraph explaining why Fell Beck flows first on the surface and then underground.

A walk in the Dales

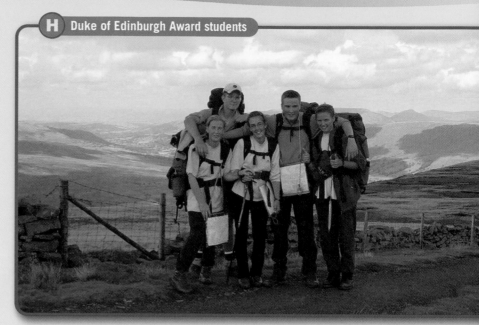

Many people enjoy hiking across the limestone scenery of the Yorkshire Dales. In August 2000 a group of students chose this area for their 75 kilometre expedition for the Duke of Edinburgh's Gold Award. They had to complete a four-day venture across some of the best limestone scenery in the country. Extract **I** from their route card shows the last 6.5 km of their walk for Day 3.

Gina, Claire, Helen, James and Steven decided to walk in this area so that they could find out more about the landscape. As part of the follow-up they plan to produce a report about their walk. Along this particular route to Malham they passed many limestone features and saw a river disappear underground and then reappear again.

Their route can be followed on map **J**. It is a 1:25 000 OS map and shows lots of detail, so the group didn't get lost! Two checkpoints are labelled: the parking area (893658) and the campsite (899633). Their route has been highlighted in **J** to make it easier to follow.

AWARD GROUP: Gina, Claire, Helen, Steven, James Cockshut Hill Technology College Gold D of E						DAY 3	DATE 31st August

Place with Grid Reference	Direction or bearing as required	Distance (km)	Time estimated	Time for meals, stops, etc.	Time for leg	ROUTE INFORMATION
START Home Farm GR 885 674 TO Footpath and road junction CHECKPOINT G GR 893 658	SE	2.7	52 min	5 min	57 min	Turn right out of Home Farm onto a track. Follow it until forest boundary. Path joins with Pennine Way and enters forest. Keep Malham Tarn to the right and follow it round, keeping to footpath closest to the river (i.e. turn right at footpath and track junctions). Carry straight on, taking the footpath directly ahead coming off the Pennine Way. Follow the path, at crossroads turn right and head towards the car park. Path joins with the road.
TO Campsite CHECKPOINT H GR 899 633	S	3.8	1 hr 04 min	10 min	1 hr 14 min	Here turn right onto road and cross the river before taking left path. At the junction take the right footpath (not the Pennine Way). At fork turn left. Pass Dean Scar. Take left path onto Pennine Way. Walk past Ing Scar Crag and down onto Malham Cove (steep descent), turn right at path junction and cross footbridge coming off the Pennine Way taking left path at fork. Follow path to campsite.

I Route card for the students' expedition

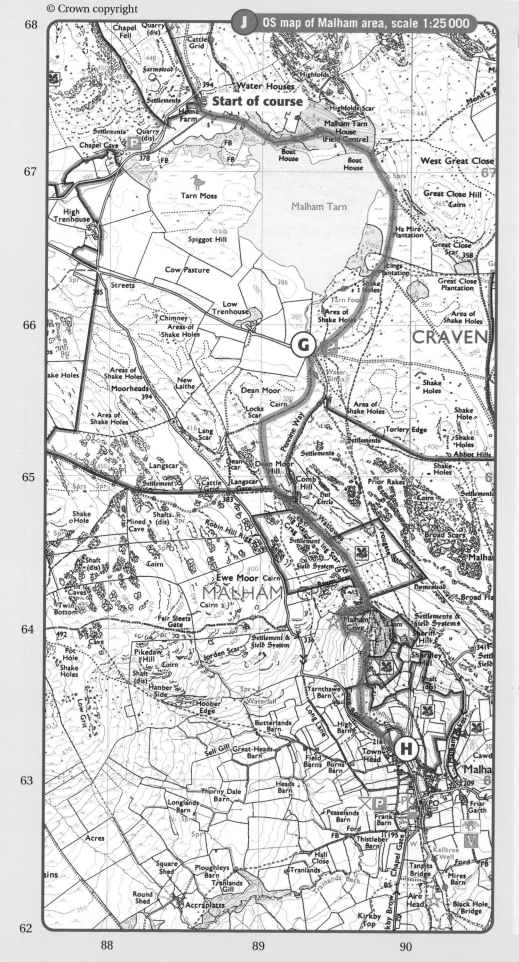

© Crown copyright

J OS map of Malham area, scale 1:25 000

Activities

Can you help the expedition group to complete their report?

6 First, look at their route card. Follow their instructions on the map so that you know which way they went.

7 Read the list of limestone features below. Write them down in the order that the group would see them on their walk.

- ◎ Water Sinks (where Malham Beck river disappears)
- ◎ Watlowes dry valley
- ◎ Malham Tarn (lake formed on slate rock)
- ◎ Malham Cove (a limestone scar)
- ◎ Shake Holes (holes where water can disappear)
- ◎ Resurgence at the foot of Malham Cove (where the river flows overland again)
- ◎ Scars (e.g. Ing Scar and Raven Scar)

8 Find each feature and give it a grid reference. Decide whether to use a four-figure reference or a six-figure grid reference for each feature – some features will cover whole grid squares while others are just in one spot.

9 Use your list to write a short presentation that the group could give about the limestone scenery they saw on their route. You should use the grid references, sketches of the features and perhaps include distances and direction details from the route card. Use the information in this unit to help you. Present your work on paper or OHP transparencies, or as a Powerpoint presentation. ICT

How is the limestone landscape being changed ?

The Yorkshire Dales National Park Authority (YDNPA) has a very important **conservation** job to do. It must protect and preserve the landscape for future generations to enjoy. The National Park covers a huge area (1773 km^2). Much of the land is privately owned and is mainly used for farming. The park has over eight million visitors each year, so a lot of pressure is put on the landscape. The National Park Authority has to make sure that the decisions they make will benefit everybody. You can see some of the challenges faced by the YDNPA in diagram **K**.

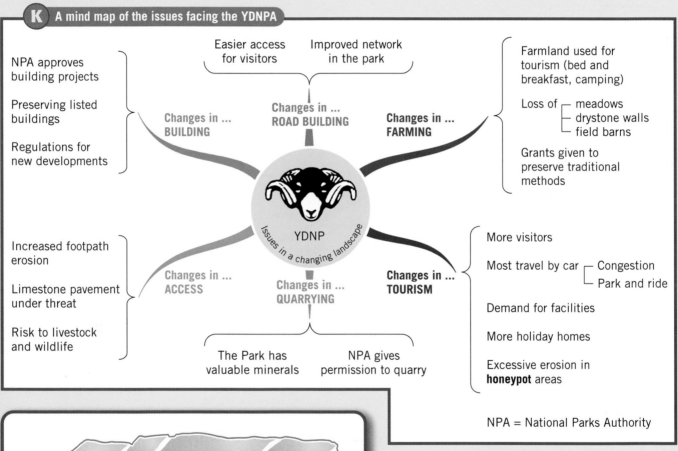

K A mind map of the issues facing the YDNPA

NPA approves building projects

Preserving listed buildings

Regulations for new developments

Changes in ... BUILDING

Easier access for visitors

Improved network in the park

Changes in ... ROAD BUILDING

Changes in ... FARMING

Farmland used for tourism (bed and breakfast, camping)

Loss of ⎯ meadows ⎯ drystone walls ⎯ field barns

Grants given to preserve traditional methods

YDNP
Issues in a changing landscape

Increased footpath erosion

Limestone pavement under threat

Risk to livestock and wildlife

Changes in ... ACCESS

Changes in ... QUARRYING

Changes in ... TOURISM

The Park has valuable minerals

NPA gives permission to quarry

More visitors

Most travel by car ⎯ Congestion ⎯ Park and ride

Demand for facilities

More holiday homes

Excessive erosion in **honeypot** areas

NPA = National Parks Authority

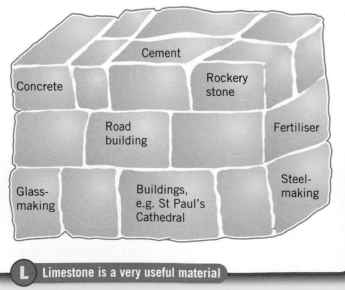

L Limestone is a very useful material

Cement

Concrete

Rockery stone

Road building

Fertiliser

Glass-making

Buildings, e.g. St Paul's Cathedral

Steel-making

The Yorkshire Dales National Park's most important asset is undoubtedly its limestone scenery. Limestone areas are important **habitats**. Many species of plants and animals can only be found in this alkaline environment, for example lime-loving plants like the birds eye primrose and rock rose. But because limestone has many uses, the scenery is under threat (**L**).

What can be done to protect limestone areas for the future?

Every five years the YDNPA is required by law to produce a National Park Management Plan. The plan includes sections about conserving the special landscape and ecology of the National Park:

- the farming landscape with its dry stone walls and traditional methods
- the archaeological sites
- the woodland areas
- the wildlife
- the limestone itself, which is an important mineral as well as a unique rock which creates spectacular scenery.

M Walkers put pressure on the limestone landscape they enjoy

Some limestone areas, like the one around Malham Tarn and Malham Cove (look back at pages 94–96), receive extra protection from conservation agencies. For example, English Nature have made this area into a **Site of Special Scientific Interest**. This means that the landscape is protected and is classified as one of the nation's most precious natural assets. The limestone pavement on the top of Malham Cove is protected by a Limestone Pavement Order so that the rock cannot be removed.

The Malham area is one of the most popular places to visit in the National Park. The number of visitors to the National Park visitor centre in Malham is recorded. Many of these people walk to the Cove and limestone pavement. During the 1990s the numbers went up steadily to around 150 000 each year– that's a potential 300 000 feet trampling the footpaths and limestone pavement!

N Some plants need a limestone habitat

Activity

12 Design a notice board for visitors to the Malham area.

- Include background information about the area.
- Explain why it is a sensitive area.
- Make sure that you include details about conservation and how the general public can help.

The writing frame could help you to write in a persuasive way.

You could use a word-processing or publishing package to help you design your poster.

> The Malham area is special because …
>
> The limestone needs to be protected for the future. This is because … and also …
>
> The public can help by … and making sure that … so that the landscape isn't destroyed.

Review and reflect

What do you know about limestone?

In this unit you have looked at limestone landscapes in England. Limestone is a unique rock that gives rise to many spectacular features. Some of the best examples of limestone pavement, swallow holes, caves and caverns are found in the Yorkshire Dales National Park. Limestone is under threat from **economic activities** that take place in the landscape, such as farming, quarrying and tourism. These landscapes are being protected by conservation orders to make sure that they survive into the future.

The Yorkshire Dales is one example of an area in Europe with superb limestone features. Photographs **A** and **B** show the Karst region of Croatia, an area so famous for its limestone scenery that it has given its name to this kind of landscape.

B Limestone in Hvar, Croatia

A Karst region of Croatia

Activities

1 Imagine that you have received email **C** from a student who lives in the Karst region of Croatia. Reply to Savo, answering all his questions and including some references for him to follow up.

> **C**
>
> Hi! My name is Savo and I live in Zagreb, Croatia. There is a wonderful area of limestone scenery near my home with lots of superb caves and caverns and fantastic limestone pavements. You have to be very careful that you don't fall down a swallow hole if you go for a walk!
>
> I've heard that there's a place in England that's just as spectacular ... the Yorkshire Dales. Could you write back and tell me all about it? What are the names of some of the best features? Where exactly are they? How can I find out more about it? Could you recommend some good websites for me to look at?
>
> Write soon!
> Savo :-)

2 As a final review of what you have learned, try this Odd One Out activity with a partner.

a Take each set of words A–F in turn and work out which word is the odd one out. Explain why, and what the others have in common.

b Next, try adding another word to each of the six groups, keeping the same odd one out.

c Finally, look through this unit again. Create your own odd one out words and groupings to test your friends!

Set A:	14	2	4
Set B:	11	8	12
Set C:	5	18	17
Set D:	7	1	3
Set E:	10	14	1
Set F:	9	18	2

1	Limestone pavement	**7**	Grykes	**14**	Impermeable
2	Joints	**8**	Swallow hole	**15**	Springs
3	Bedding planes	**9**	Sedimentary	**16**	Caverns
4	Permeable	**10**	Karst	**17**	Calcium carbonate
5	Precipitation	**11**	Stalactites	**18**	Chemical weathering
6	Clints	**12**	Stalagmites		
		13	Caves		

7 Can the Earth cope?

Ecosystems, population and resources

A Smoke emissions in New Orleans, USA

B The problem of waste: Stockton-on-Tees, UK

C Deforestation in Johor State, Malaysia

D Rock slide following an earthquake, India

Learn about

The world's growing population and its demand for resources have many consequences for the environment. This unit will help you investigate ecosystems, population and resources, and how they are linked together. You will explore:

- what ecosystems are and where they are found
- how vegetation is related to climate, soil and human activity
- how population and resources are linked
- how a resource can best be managed
- what the future is for global resources.

E Confiscated ivory being burned in Kenya

The Earth is a fragile planet, but there are many ways in which it can protect and maintain itself. For example, the **ozone layer** protects it against harmful rays from the Sun. The Earth's oceans and forests can absorb excess carbon dioxide (CO_2) produced by burning **fossil fuels**. Diagram **F** shows how different parts of the Earth's environment are linked together to maintain a living planet.

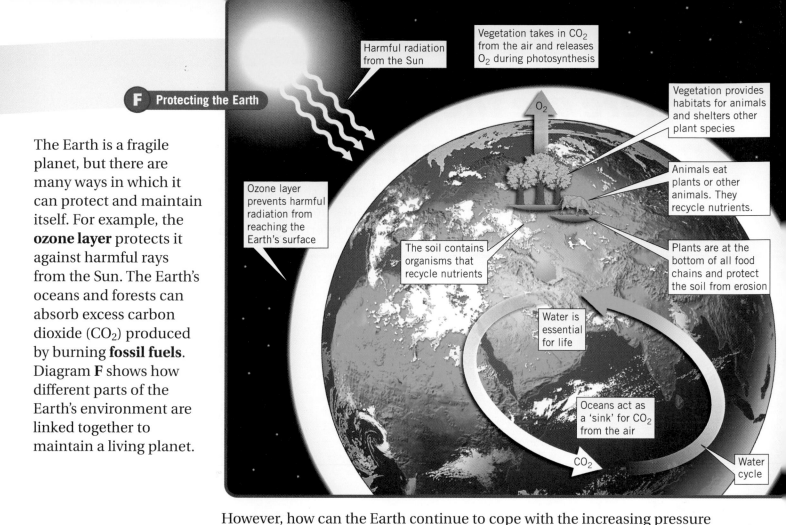

Harmful radiation from the Sun

Vegetation takes in CO_2 from the air and releases O_2 during photosynthesis

Vegetation provides habitats for animals and shelters other plant species

Animals eat plants or other animals. They recycle nutrients.

Ozone layer prevents harmful radiation from reaching the Earth's surface

The soil contains organisms that recycle nutrients

Plants are at the bottom of all food chains and protect the soil from erosion

Water is essential for life

Oceans act as a 'sink' for CO_2 from the air

CO_2

Water cycle

However, how can the Earth continue to cope with the increasing pressure put on it by human beings? The world's population continues to grow at an alarming rate: approximately 1.6 million more people a week in 2001. This growing population consumes more and more of the Earth's resources, for food, clothing and shelter, as well as to make a huge range of other goods.

Activities

1   In a small group, discuss ways in which the Earth is able to protect itself. Diagram **F** will help you. Use the points in the table, as well as adding your own.

Parts of the environment	How they help to protect and maintain the Earth
Vegetation (**flora**)	
Soil	
Water	
Animals (**fauna**)	
The atmosphere	

3   **Extension**

Investigate environmental incidents in the news using newspapers, TV or the Internet. Add them to your list in **2**, then present a summary of your findings. You can find useful information on websites listed at www.heinemann.co.uk/hotlinks (insert code 5171P). ICT

2   Study the environmental incidents shown in the photographs, and use an atlas to find their locations. Then copy and complete this table.

Photograph and what it shows	Country where the incident took place	Continent	Populated area (Yes or No)	Part of the Earth *most* affected (vegetation, soil, water, animals, atmosphere)
A				
B				

Where are the Earth's major ecosystems?

The Earth is made up of many different **ecosystems**. Map **A** shows the world distribution of three types of ecosystems: tropical rainforest ecosystems, hot desert ecosystems and coral reef ecosystems. An ecosystem on a global scale is often referred to as a **biome**.

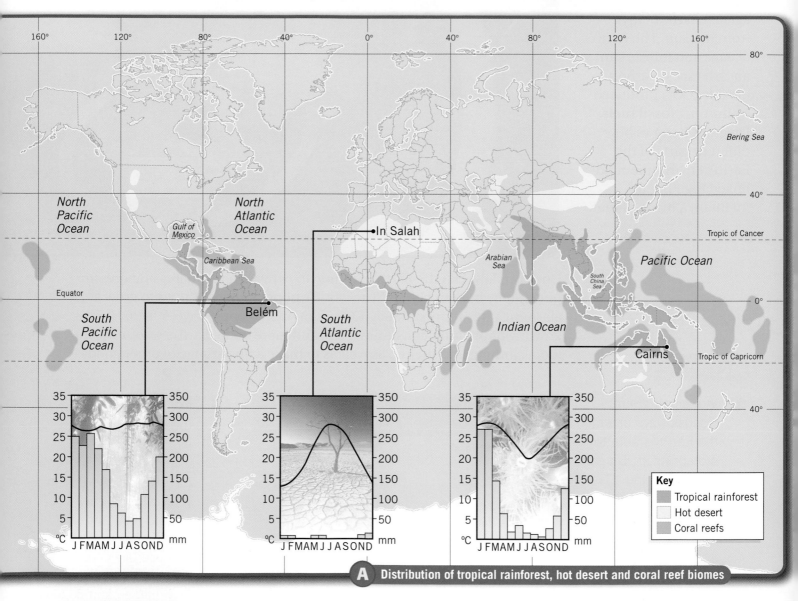

A Distribution of tropical rainforest, hot desert and coral reef biomes

Key
- Tropical rainforest
- Hot desert
- Coral reefs

Getting Technical ▼

- ⚙ An **ecosystem** is a community of plants and animals and the environment they live in. Each part of the ecosystem depends on the other parts. An ecosystem includes **flora** (plants), **fauna** (animals), climate and soil.
- ⚙ A **biome** is the biggest ecological unit. It consists of a group of related ecosystems that share the same kind of special plant life and climate.
- ⚙ A **community** is a group of plants and animals living closely together.

How does vegetation adapt to its environment?

Plants develop special features to survive and make the most of their environment. These features are called **adaptations**. They allow a plant to cope with too much water or too little, too much heat or cold, windy or calm conditions. The diagrams in **B** show some examples of adaptations made by plants in a variety of biomes.

Spines of a cactus plant – in dry climates, these lose less water through **evapotranspiration** than leaves.

Long root systems just beneath the soil – plants in hot, dry environments need to use any rain that falls immediately.

Buttress roots – in a tropical rainforest, trees grow to great heights to compete for sunlight and air. The large buttress roots support the tall trees.

Leaves with **drip tips** – in very wet climates the drip tips allow rainwater to run off the leaf quickly, before the plant is damaged by the weight of water that may collect.

B These plants show adaptations to a variety of environmental conditions

Activities

1 In pairs, investigate either tropical rainforest or hot desert in more detail. Follow these steps and use **A** to prepare a guide to your biome.

   a Describe its world distribution.

   b Use an atlas to find three named examples of your chosen biome.

   c Name the continents or oceans and some countries where the biome is found. It may be on the land or in the waters around those countries.

   d Use the photograph in **A** to describe or sketch the vegetation.

   e Use the graph in **A** to describe the climate at different times of the year.

2 **a** Design and draw a perfect plant that would flourish in your chosen biome. Use the adaptations shown in **B** as a starting point.

help!

Try to use some of these terms in your answers:

- Northern Hemisphere/ Southern Hemisphere
- Equator
- Tropics
- coastal
- interior
- even/uneven
- scattered
- clustered.

   b Annotate your diagram to show how your plant would adapt to the conditions in the biome. Think about the difficulties it may face from the climate, other flora, fauna and the soil.

3 **Extension**

Find the map of world vegetation in your atlas. Choose a different biome to investigate and compare it to your work in activity **1**.

How are ecosystems linked to human activity?

An ecosystem is a **community** of plants and animals which exist together under similar conditions, such as climate and soil. Diagram **A** helps you to understand what an ecosystem is and how the four parts of an ecosystem are closely interconnected.

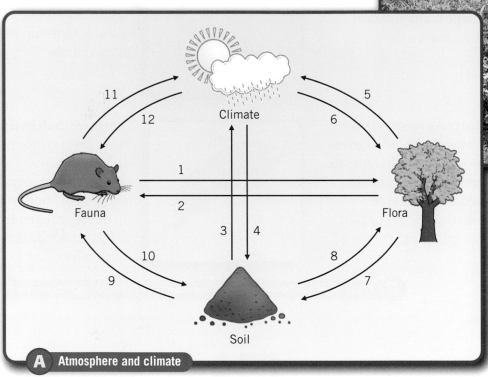

A Atmosphere and climate

B The Amazonian rainforest ecosystem

Most ecosystems are affected by human activity. People need to use and modify the natural environment to help them survive, for example to grow food, provide shelter, or extract resources such as coal or precious metals. Activity **3** will help you explore these **impacts**. However, if the Earth is to cope with the demands that are made on it, people need to realise that many of its resources are not renewable – they will run out. Humans will have to use and manage the Earth's resources in a more **sustainable** way.

Getting Technical ▼

- ⓢ **Renewable resource:** a resource which can be used again and again, for example trees, which can be replanted, or wind, which can be used to make electricity

- ⓢ **Non-renewable resource:** a resource which will never be replaced once it is used, for example soil

- ⓢ **Sustainable development:** using resources wisely today, so that people in the future can still use them. To be sustainable, renewable resources must be allowed to regenerate, and alternatives must be found for non-renewable resources

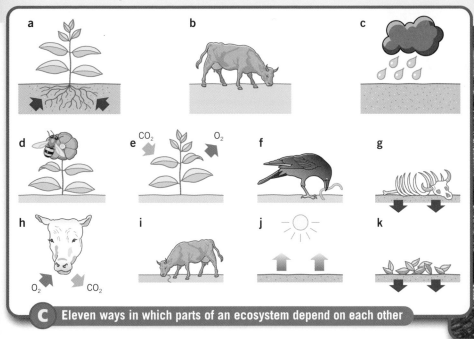

C Eleven ways in which parts of an ecosystem depend on each other

D Human impacts on ecosystem in Amazonia

Activities

1 **a** Draw a sketch of a tropical rainforest.

   b Use diagram **A** to label the four main parts of the ecosystem on your sketch.

   c Add arrows copied from diagram **A** to show how the different parts of the ecosystem are linked.

2 Look at diagram **A** and the sketches in **C**.

   a Make a copy of the table below.

   b Match the sketches **a–k** in **C** to the numbered arrows 1 to 12 in **A**. Some sketches match two numbers.

   c Describe what each link shows.

   d Write a short summary of what you have found out about ecosystems.

Arrow number (1–12)	Matches with sketch (a–k)	Description of the link
1	d	A bee pollinates the flower of a plant
2		

3 Photograph **D** shows the effects of human activity on an ecosystem.

   a Work in pairs at first for this activity. First discuss which ecosystem is shown in **D**, and how human activity has changed it. It may help you to write notes on rough paper.

   b Use diagram **A** to discuss how changes will affect the fauna, flora, soil and climate in this ecosystem.

For example:

> By cutting down the trees, people have removed protection from the soil. This allows rain to wash the soil away …

   c Write a paragraph to describe and explain the impact people have had on this ecosystem. Include the following information:

   - name and location of ecosystem
   - the change brought about by human activity
   - the effects on fauna
   - the effects on flora
   - the effects on soil
   - the effects on climate.

help!

Remember that:

- good descriptions include details or examples
- good explanations say why things change – they use linking words like *why, because,* and *so*.

4 Humans need to use ecosystems to survive. Try to think of ways in which we can use the Earth's ecosystems while causing as little damage as possible. You could start by thinking of how to use the ecosystem in photograph **D** in a more sustainable way.

How do ecosystems work?

All living things need energy to exist. Animals such as humans get their energy by eating plants or other animals, but plants can make their own energy. They take water from the soil, and use carbon dioxide from the atmosphere and sunlight to produce the energy they need. This process takes place in the green leaves of plants and is called **photosynthesis**.

Photosynthesis happens faster where there is plenty of sunlight, high temperatures and enough moisture. So photosynthesis produces more energy in some parts of the world than in others, and plants are able to grow faster (photos **D–H**).

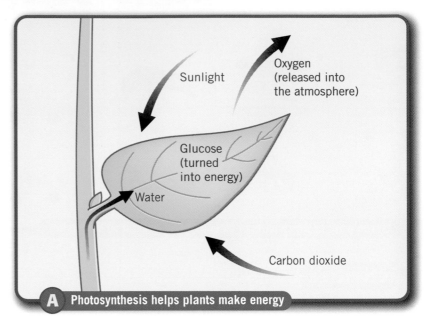

A Photosynthesis helps plants make energy

The energy plants produce is essential to other living things. Some animals get their energy from eating plants, and they are eaten by other animals. So the energy plants make flows through a **food chain** to other parts of the ecosystem (see **B**).

The total amount of energy plants produce in an ecosystem is called **primary productivity**. Ecosystems with high productivity have more species of plants and animals, because there is more energy available to support them.

How nutrients are recycled

Plants and animals need **nutrients** as well as energy to grow. Plants take nutrients from the soil through their roots. These nutrients move through the food chain and are recycled back into the soil. For example, when plants and animals die, they are broken down by bacteria and fungi (see **C**). Nutrients are recycled much more quickly in parts of the world with warm, wet climates than in cold or dry climates. Where nutrients are recycled quickly, they are stored in the vegetation, and the soils can become poor.

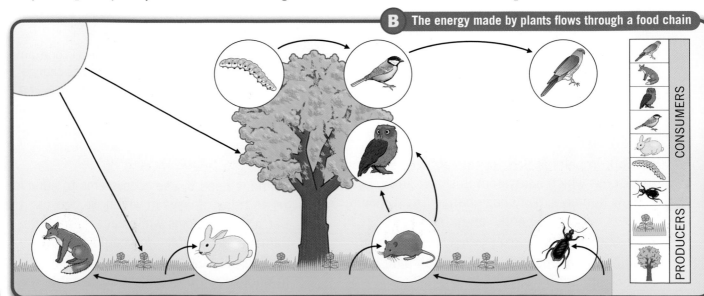

B The energy made by plants flows through a food chain

CONSUMERS

PRODUCERS

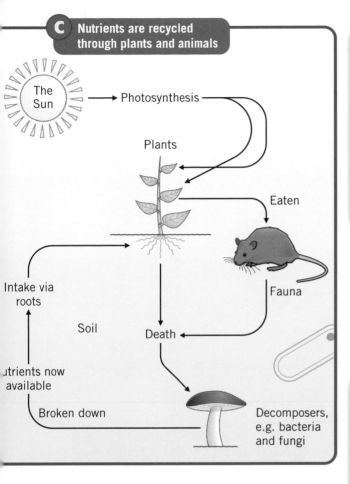

C Nutrients are recycled through plants and animals

D Tropical rainforest

E Hot desert

F Temperate grassland

H Tundra

G Tropical savannah

Activities

1 **a** On a copy of figure **A**, underline the inputs to photosynthesis in one colour, and the outputs in a different colour.

    b Next to each input, label where the plant gets it from.

    c Now write a sentence or two explaining the process of photosynthesis in your own words.

2 **a** Find a world map of vegetation types in your atlas. Find the ecosystems shown in photographs **D** to **H**.

    b Make a list of the ecosystems. You could set your work out in a table like the one below.

    c Study the photographs and find out about their climates. Decide which ecosystems will have the highest rate of photosynthesis.

Ecosystem	Climate	Photosynthesis	Reasons
Tropical rainforest	Hot and wet most of the year	High	High temperatures and rainfall

    d Now decide which ecosystems will have low or medium rates of photosynthesis. Explain your choices.

3 Choose ecosystems from photographs **D** to **H** where you think nutrient cycling would be fast, medium or slow.

4 Check that you understand the definitions of the key words in **bold**, then add them to your geography word bank. 📖

5 **Extension**

    Write a short summary explaining what you have found out about how ecosystems in different parts of the world work, or label what you have found out onto a world map.

How are population and resources linked?

As you have seen, the world's growing population uses more and more of the Earth's resources. However, people in different parts of the world do not have equal access to the world's natural resources. For example:

⊚ the richest 20 per cent of the world's population use 80 per cent of the resources

⊚ the richest 20 per cent of the world's population own 85 per cent of the wealth

⊚ 80 per cent of the world's population live in LEDCs.

One reason is that natural resources are not found evenly throughout the world (**C**). Another is that wealthier countries have the power and money to gain a bigger share of the world's resources through trade (you will find out more about this in *Geography Matters 3*). For example, wealthy countries such as Japan with few natural resources buy resources from poorer countries with more resources. The population of the USA uses more of the Earth's resources than any other country. Unlike Japan, it has many resources of its own.

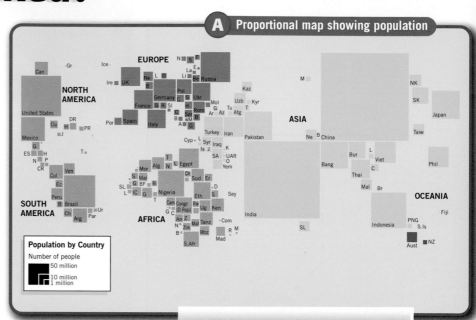

A Proportional map showing population

Population by Country
Number of people
50 million
10 million
1 million

Getting Technical ▼

Proportional maps

A **proportional map** uses a value, such as GDP, to map the world, rather than land area. So Switzerland, which looks small on a traditional map, looks big because it has a high GNP.

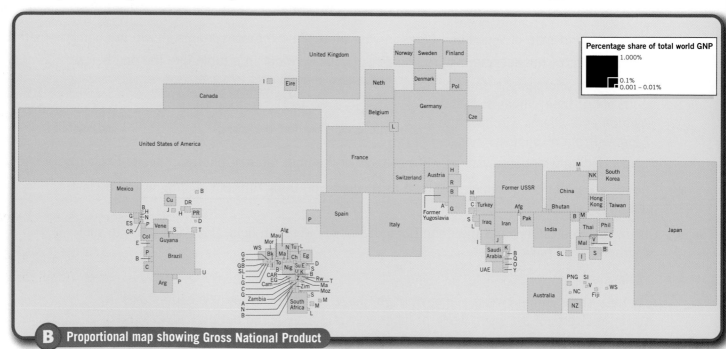

B Proportional map showing Gross National Product

Percentage share of total world GNP
1.000%
0.1%
0.001 – 0.01%

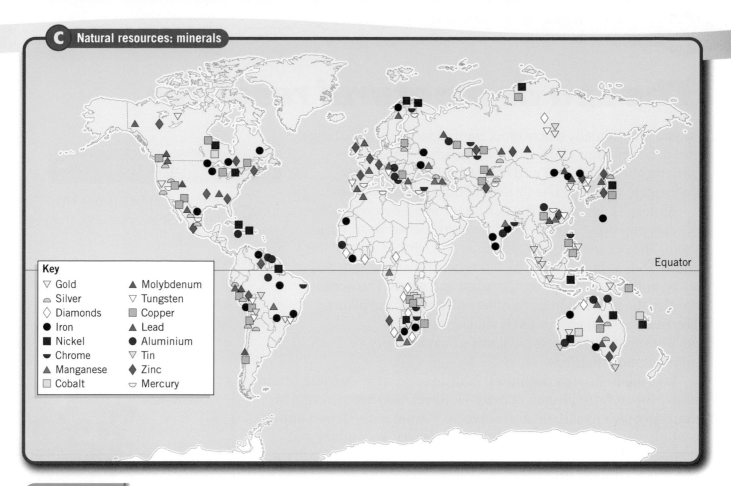

C Natural resources: minerals

Equator

Key

▽ Gold	▲ Molybdenum
⌂ Silver	▽ Tungsten
◇ Diamonds	▣ Copper
● Iron	▲ Lead
■ Nickel	● Aluminium
◡ Chrome	▽ Tin
▲ Manganese	◆ Zinc
□ Cobalt	◡ Mercury

Activities

1 The purpose of this activity is to get you thinking about natural resources. Work in pairs.

   a Think carefully about a room at home or in school. Imagine you are taking a video camera into the room. Pan the camera around the room and think of all the objects you can see. It may help if you close your eyes.

   b In turn, describe what you saw to your partner while they note all the objects down.

   c Discuss which natural resources were used to make each object. List them next to the object.

help! Some household goods include hundreds of parts made of many different resources. You could aim for variety in your list, or investigate one object in more detail. You could then share your ideas with the rest of the class to get one large list.

2 Discuss which resources are **renewable** and which are **non-renewable**. Colour code your list into these two groups.

3 Use maps **A** and **B** and an atlas to find:

   ⚅ a wealthy region of the world with a high population

   ⚅ a poor region of the world with a high population

   ⚅ a poor region of the world with a low population

   ⚅ a wealthy part of the world with a low population.

4 Work in pairs or groups of three.

   a Choose one resource each from map **C**, and investigate the distribution of the resource – use these questions to help you.

   ⚅ Which continents or countries is it mainly found in?

   ⚅ Which parts of the world lack the resource?

   ⚅ Is the resource found in parts of the world where many people live?

   ⚅ Is the resource found in parts of the world which have a high, medium or low GDP?

   b Compare your results with those of your partner. What are the main similarities and differences between the resources?

   c Produce a world outline map showing the distribution of your resources. Annotate it to show your findings.

5 Add the key words in **bold** on these two pages to your word bank. 📖

The sea as a natural resource

As you have already discovered, natural resources are things you use every day. They can be found above ground, underground, in the air and in water. These two pages investigate the natural resources of our seas and oceans.

Almost 71 per cent of the Earth's surface is covered by the oceans, and over 97 per cent of the Earth's water is stored in them. The oceans have a huge impact on climate around the globe. They supply water which reaches the land as rain and snow, and influence the temperature and winds. The oceans are also the home of huge numbers of animals and plants. The **marine** (sea) ecosystem is vital to the Earth's environment – without it the Earth would be a very different place to live.

Like all the Earth's resources, marine ecosystems are fragile and under threat from human activity. However, they are also vital for many people's livelihood and survival. Marine ecosystems support a whole range of economic activities, **primary**, **secondary** and **tertiary**. Even for people who do not have direct contact with the sea, it is an important resource.

Photographs **A–F** show a variety of ways in which people use marine ecosystems as a resource.

Getting Technical ▾

- A **primary** activity is one that takes a natural resource from the Earth.
- A **secondary** activity is one that makes a product from resources.
- A **tertiary** activity provides a service to people.

A People enjoying the seaside at South Bay, Scarborough, UK

C Japanese whaling in the Southern Ocean

D An oil rig in the North Sea

B Fishing trawler, Bering Sea

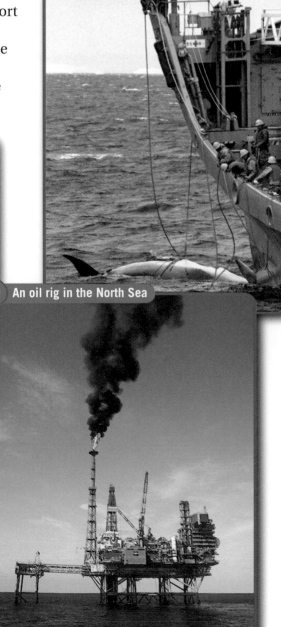

E Diving off the coast of Kenya

F Fish grading in Orkney, Scotland

Activities

1 **a** With a partner, study photographs **A** to **F**, then discuss the different ways they show people using the sea as a resource.

b Copy the table below. For each photograph, describe at least one way in which the sea is being used.

c Decide whether each activity is primary, secondary or tertiary, then add an explanation to your table. One example has been done for you.

hint

Be careful – there may not be a simple answer for some of these photographs. It all depends on the reason you give.

Photograph	Location	How the sea is used as a resource	Primary, secondary or tertiary activity
F	Scotland	The photo shows the sea is being used as a source of food for people.	This is a secondary activity because the fish will be made into products like fish cakes.

2 **a** Work in pairs. Choose three of the photographs you have investigated. Work out ways in which the activities they show may have an impact on the marine ecosystem. Share your ideas with another pair.

b Using the photographs to help you, list the ways you or your families use the sea as a resource. Are there any links between your use of the resources and impacts on the environment?

3 Use the photographs and your work so far to look for resource chains that link natural resources and the people who consume them. You can see one example, partly complete, in the table. Try to think of at least one more.

Resource	Primary activity	Secondary activity	Tertiary activity	Consumer
Fish		Fish factory		People eating fish products

4 Use the Oceans Alive website listed at www.heinemann.co.uk/hotlinks (insert code 5171P) and other resources from a library or newspapers to produce a leaflet or poster explaining to the reader how and why the sea is an important resource. You could use a wordprocessing or DTP package to present your work. (ICT)

Threats to marine ecosystems

Seas and oceans cover over two-thirds of the Earth's surface, so it is not surprising that they have become polluted as a result of human activities. Polluted water and waste materials are dumped directly into the sea, flow into the sea from rivers, or fall from the atmosphere. Table **A** shows the main sources of marine pollution.

Source		Pollutants	Percentage of total
Atmosphere		Particles blown by the wind, and gases from industry and vehicles	33%
Run-off and discharges from the land		Sewage and waste from farms and industry	44%
Ships		Oil spills and leaks, and cargo spills	12%
Dumping at sea		Waste from dredging, sewage sludge, and ships' garbage	10%
Offshore oil and gas production		Waste from oil and gas drilling	1%

A Sources of marine pollution

People are often surprised that oil spills make up such a small percentage of marine pollution. When an oil spill occurs, it is very visible and some of the impacts are almost immediate. However, run-off and discharges from the land are more widespread and are harder to trace.

The oil industry

Oil is one of the most valuable resources which people **extract** from the environment. **Crude oil** was formed many millions of years ago, so it is a **non-renewable resource**. It is found in rocks beneath the land and some of the Earth's seas.

As well as extracting oil from the seas and oceans, we also transport oil by sea to where it will be **refined** and used. Pipelines and huge tankers carry oil across the world. Map **C** shows the world's major oilfields and the network of oil shipping lanes which link the producers of oil with the countries which **consume** it. However, producing and transporting oil puts the world's marine ecosystems at risk from oil pollution (see **B**).

Getting Technical ▼

⊚ **Pollution:** when harmful substances make the air, land or water dirty

⊚ **Pollutant:** a harmful substance that causes pollution, such as exhaust fumes.

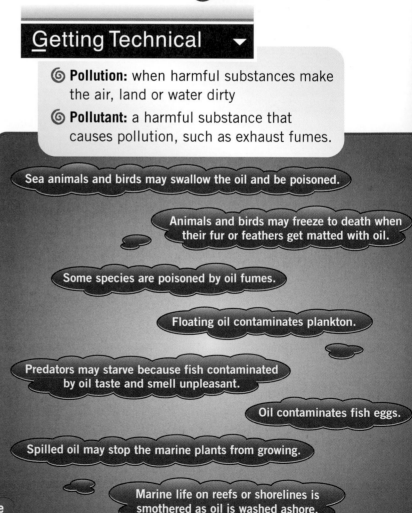

Sea animals and birds may swallow the oil and be poisoned.

Animals and birds may freeze to death when their fur or feathers get matted with oil.

Some species are poisoned by oil fumes.

Floating oil contaminates plankton.

Predators may starve because fish contaminated by oil taste and smell unpleasant.

Oil contaminates fish eggs.

Spilled oil may stop the marine plants from growing.

Marine life on reefs or shorelines is smothered as oil is washed ashore.

B Effects of oil on the marine ecosystem

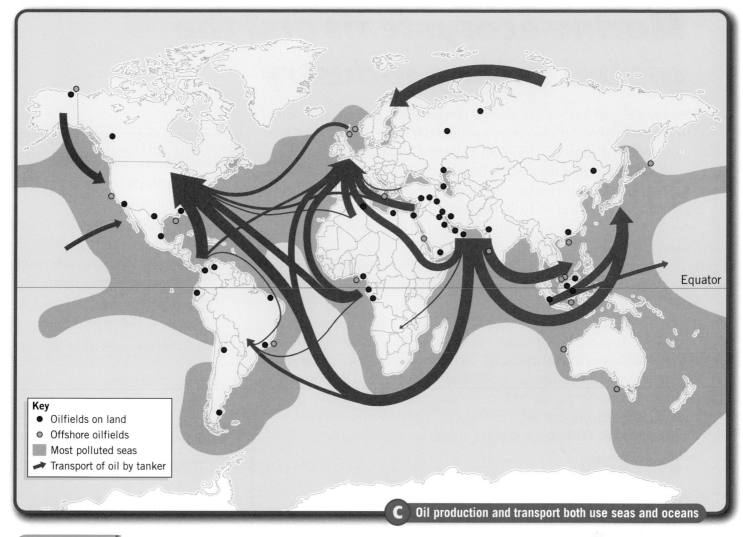

Key
- ● Oilfields on land
- ○ Offshore oilfields
- ▨ Most polluted seas
- ➤ Transport of oil by tanker

Equator

C Oil production and transport both use seas and oceans

Activities

1 Draw a graph to show the data in table **A**. Choose the type of graph you use carefully. Add a title and a key.

2 Study diagram **B**, which shows the impact of oil on a marine ecosystem.

  a Choose the impact that you think would affect the marine ecosystem most quickly. Explain your choice.

  b Which of the impacts do you think would take the longest to affect the marine ecosystem?

3 Use map **C** and an atlas to investigate the seas and oceans where the threat of oil pollution is greatest.

  a Find the world's biggest oil-producing area, and the three parts of the world which consume most oil.

  b List the seas or oceans where offshore oilfields are located.

  c List the oceans and seas most at risk from accidents or spills from oil tankers.

4 Map **C** also shows the most polluted seas in the world.

  a Working in pairs, see whether you can see a link between the pattern of polluted seas and what you have found out about the risk of oil pollution. You might want to make a rough list of seas where there seems to be a link, and a list of seas where there does not seem to be a link.

  b Make a short presentation of your conclusions. Table **A** may help you explain what you have found out.

  c Look through the other world maps in your atlas. Find another map which helps you to explain more about the pattern of marine pollution.

Marine ecosystems and the global fishing industry

Fish are a vital part of the marine ecosystem. They are also one of the most important resources people take from the sea. Fish are an important source of food, and about 12.5 million people around the world earn a living from fishing. However, many of the world's seas and oceans are being **overfished**. The United Nations believe that 60 to 70 per cent of **fish stocks** are threatened worldwide, and urgent action is needed to **conserve** fish for the future.

As the world's population has grown, the demand for fish has increased rapidly. At the same time, many fishing boats have become better at catching fish, so the amount of fish caught has increased too (graph **A**). But although fish is a **renewable** resource, fish are being caught faster than they can reproduce in many **fishing grounds** (map **B**). To make matters worse, newer and larger fishing boats are patrolling the oceans. They can sail to distant seas where they find, catch and process fish much more efficiently. Traditional fishing boats in coastal waters cannot compete with these large factory ships.

Getting Technical ▾

- **Fish stock:** the total number of fish in an area
- **Overfishing:** when fish are taken out of the sea faster than they can reproduce, so the number of fish steadily goes down
- **Fishing grounds:** the parts of the oceans where fishing goes on
- **Conserve:** look after for the future

Fact file

- People in Japan eat the most fish: 72 kg per person every year.
- Other big fish-eaters are the people of Iceland and Greenland.
- The four biggest fishing nations are China, Peru, Chile and Japan. They take 42 per cent of the world's fishing catch.

A World fish production, 1950–1999

Key
— Fish farming
— Capture fisheries

1999

Fish production (million tonnes): 0, 20, 40, 60, 80, 100, 120, 140
Years: 1950, 1954, 1958, 1962, 1966, 1970, 1974, 1978, 1982, 1986, 1990, 1994, 1998

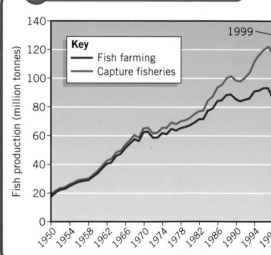

B The world's fishing grounds

Barents Sea

Grand Banks

Bahamian Marine Ecosystem

Southern Caribbean Sea

North East Brazilian Coastal Ecosystem

Mediterranean Sea

Gulf of Guinea Marine Ecosystems

Equator

Western Guinea Current Marine Ecosystem

South West Atlantic Coast Marine Ecosystem

Key
Fish consumption per person per year
- 0–10 kg
- 11–30 kg
- 31–50 kg
- 51–80 kg
- Threatened fisheries
- Fishing grounds

Ocean	Fish catch in million tonnes
North Atlantic	21
South Atlantic	4
Indian	8
Western Pacific	34.3
Eastern Pacific	18.9

C The world fish catch, 1997

Traditional fishing boats often fish quite close to land, and provide jobs for local people. They are usually too small to overfish, so they are more **sustainable** (photo **D**).

Factory ships (photo **E**) track fish down using electronic equipment and catch them using huge nets. The fish are often processed and frozen on board.

One solution to overfishing is to raise fish in fish farms (photo **F**). The fish are specially fed so they grow fast. When they are big enough, they are easy to catch. However, the waste from fish farms can pollute the surrounding water.

D Traditional fishing in Kerala, India

E Processing fish aboard a trawler in the Bering Sea

F Salmon farm in Dover, Tasmania

Activities

1 a Use the figures in table **C** and an outline map of the world. Choose a type of graph to show the weight of fish caught in each ocean. (123)

b Shade your map to show the endangered fishing grounds.

c Label the information in the fact file onto your map.

d In pairs, discuss whether you can see any links between the different sorts of information on your map.

2 a Read again about traditional fishing, modern factory ships and fish farming and look at photographs **D**, **E** and **F**. Draw up a table like the one below to help you work out the advantages and disadvantages of each sort of fishing.

	Advantages	Disadvantages
Traditional fishing boats		
Large factory ships		
Fish farming		

b Underline the advantages and disadvantages for people in blue, and those for the environment in green.

3 Using your work from activities **1** and **2**, write a short summary to explain what you have learned about the problem of overfishing. Include all the key words in **bold** to show you understand them.

4 **Extension**

Investigate overfishing and conservation from the Worldwide Fund for Nature website at their *endangered seas* page by going to www.heinemann.co.uk/hotlinks (insert code 5171P). Choose either **a** or **b** below.

a Choose one fishing problem or conservation story from the website. Make an ICT presentation by choosing images and key points from the website.

b Use an atlas to check the location of the main news stories and annotate them onto a world outline map. Then colour code your labels to show different types of story, for example problems and successes. (ICT)

Case Study
Overfishing in the North Sea

A The North Sea

The North Sea is suffering the effects of overfishing. Scientists warn that cod numbers in the North Sea are about to collapse. The World Wide Fund for Nature (WWF) go further – they say that in some places cod is actually an **endangered species**.

One reason for this is that most of the big fish have already been caught. As cod becomes harder to find, fishermen are forced to catch smaller and younger fish. Eighty per cent of the cod they catch are below breeding age, leaving fewer and fewer cod to breed for the future.

The European Union

The countries around the North Sea all belong to the European Union (EU). The EU has a difficult job; it has to:

- manage fishing fairly for the fishermen of each country

- manage fishing in a sustainable way

- help keep people in the EU supplied with fish.

There are so few mackerel it is not worth fishermen leaving port. Herring are now recovering after numbers went so low in 1995 that fishing for them was banned. Cod, haddock, plaice and prawns are heading the same way. However, this does not have to be the case. During the First and Second World Wars no fishing took place in the North Sea. For five years after the wars finished, all fish species saw healthy recoveries. This could happen again!

B The views of Amy Chang, North Sea environmentalist

Even before the fishing ban, we were struggling to make ends meet. I understand the need for conservation, but I need to catch 170 tonnes of cod a year to make a profit. Three years ago I invested £250 000 in my trawler, but our catches have gone down for the past two years. I now travel further in search of fishing grounds where I am allowed to fish, towards the coast of Holland. This will increase my costs and I'll have to be out at sea longer. This ban is too harsh and the government should compensate us.

C Sam Douglas, fisherman from the Port of Grimsby

Saving the cod

Ban on North Sea cod fishing – 24 January 2001

THE EUROPEAN COMMISSION announces that 100 000 square kilometres of the North Sea, almost 20 per cent of its entire area, will be out of bounds to boats fishing for cod, haddock, and whiting. This is a desperate attempt to ensure that there will be cod left in the North Sea next year.

The UK will be worst affected by the ban since it has the longest coastline bordering the North Sea. Britain also has a long tradition of cod fishing – British people eat one-third of the world's cod catch.

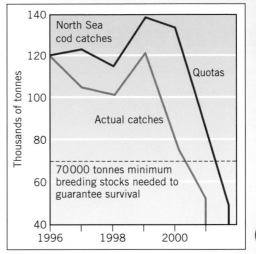

D

Conservation choices

Most people think conserving fish is a good idea, but it means making difficult decisions. These affect everybody who catches, processes or eats fish. The decisions also affect the future of the whole marine ecosystem. Ideas for conservation include:

- banning fishing from some areas of the North Sea
- a **quota** (limit) on the amount of fish that people can catch
- paying fishermen to scrap older boats
- limiting the number of days that fishermen can go fishing.

Activities

1. List the countries that border the North Sea which might want to fish there.

2. Look at figure **D**.
   a. Describe what the graph tells you about changes in North Sea cod catches.
   b. When was the last time fishermen matched the quota set by the EU? What does this tell you about cod numbers in the North Sea?

3. a. Work in pairs. Make a list of the ideas for conservation in the North Sea, then explain how they would work. Make notes in a table like the one below.

Conservation ideas	How they would work	Ranking	Ranking
Banning fishing from some areas	This would help conserve fish because …		

   b. Decide which you think would be the best idea from the point of view of fishermen. Use a blue pen and rank this idea 1, then the next best 2, and so on.
   c. Decide which you think would be the best idea from the point of view of the environmentalist. Use a green pen, and rank this idea 1, then the next best 2, and so on.
   d. Make a short presentation to explain *your* point of view. Include any ideas of your own.

Coral reefs: the 'tropical rainforests' of the sea

A Aerial view of Kuata Island, south west of Fiji

B Stone coral

Coral reefs are one of the most important ecosystems in the world. They are very **diverse** – they are home to huge numbers of different fauna and flora. Many **ecologists** call them the 'tropical rainforests' of the sea because they provide a unique habitat. Although coral reefs cover less than 1 per cent of the Earth's surface, over 25 per cent of all fish species in the ocean live in, or close to, coral reefs.

What is a coral reef?

A coral reef is made up of millions upon millions of coral **polyps**. They are the thin living layer which covers the reef. The polyps are tiny animals, but they contain plants called **algae**. The algae use photosynthesis to convert sunlight into energy – this energy is used by the coral itself. Coral reefs are very colourful because many different algae reflect different colours in the sunlight.

The coral polyps make hard calcium carbonate. Over thousands of years this builds up and forms the massive reefs seen in places like the Great Barrier Reef in Australia.

Getting Technical ▼

🌀 **Biodiversity:** the number of different species of plants and animals in an ecosystem. Human activity has reduced the world's biodiversity, with some species of plants and animals becoming extinct.

E Conditions that encourage coral growth

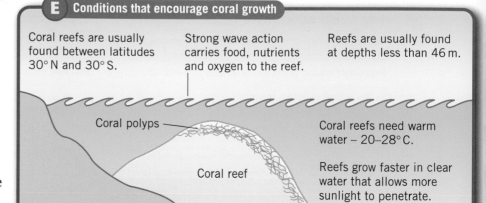

Coral reefs are usually found between latitudes 30° N and 30° S.

Strong wave action carries food, nutrients and oxygen to the reef.

Reefs are usually found at depths less than 46 m.

Coral polyps

Coral reef

Coral reefs need warm water – 20–28° C.

Reefs grow faster in clear water that allows more sunlight to penetrate.

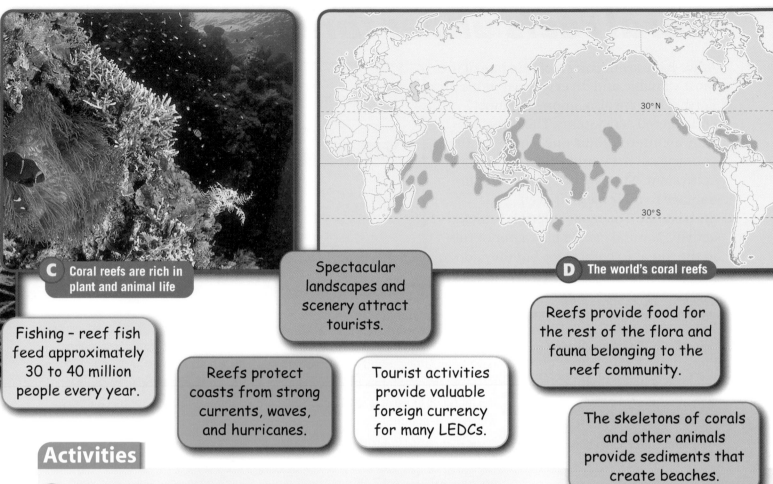

C Coral reefs are rich in plant and animal life

Spectacular landscapes and scenery attract tourists.

D The world's coral reefs

30° N

30° S

Fishing – reef fish feed approximately 30 to 40 million people every year.

Reefs protect coasts from strong currents, waves, and hurricanes.

Tourist activities provide valuable foreign currency for many LEDCs.

Reefs provide food for the rest of the flora and fauna belonging to the reef community.

The skeletons of corals and other animals provide sediments that create beaches.

Activities

1. Some people say coral reefs are like the tropical rainforests of the sea.

   a Make a copy of the table below. Then put each of the words and phrases beneath the table in the correct column. The information on pages 75 and 108 may help you.

Coral reefs only	Tropical rainforests only	Both coral reefs and tropical rainforests

   - Located within the tropics
   - Colourful
   - Rich in animal and plant life
   - Create spectacular scenery
   - Take many years to grow and mature
   - Use photosynthesis to make energy
   - Are under threat from human activity
   - Provide work for local people
   - Protect the soil
   - Shelter fish
   - Easy to find out about in newspapers, magazines, and on TV

   b Which, if any, did you find difficult to place in your table? Briefly explain your answer.

   c Think of some words and phrases of your own to add to your table.

   d Do you think that 'tropical rainforests of the sea' is a helpful description of coral reefs?

2. Using the Internet and other sources, collect information on different coral reefs around the world. Compare them by completing a table like the one below. You could add columns of your own to this table. Go to www.heinemann.co.uk/hotlinks (insert code 5171P) for a useful website. ICT

Location of coral reef	Main features / Description of coral reef	Main threats to the coral reef

125

Coral reefs under threat

As we have seen, coral reefs are one of the most valuable and **diverse** ecosystems on Earth. They are also among the most endangered ecosystems. The threat is truly an international one. There are 109 countries in the world with a coral reef ecosystem. Ninety-three of these report damage to their reefs, or even destruction. The main culprit is human activity. Natural causes play a minor role in the threat to coral reefs, but they add to the damage caused by human activity.

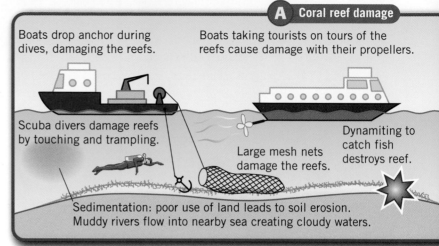

A Coral reef damage

Boats drop anchor during dives, damaging the reefs.

Boats taking tourists on tours of the reefs cause damage with their propellers.

Scuba divers damage reefs by touching and trampling.

Large mesh nets damage the reefs.

Dynamiting to catch fish destroys reef.

Sedimentation: poor use of land leads to soil erosion. Muddy rivers flow into nearby sea creating cloudy waters.

Natural threat to coral reef	Summary of threat
The effects of climate change	Changes in weather patterns cause problems for reef ecosystems. Hurricanes have been stronger and more frequent recently, which may be partly due to global warming. Storms have devastating effects on the coral reefs because of the increase in wave energy. Also sediment generated during storms can bury whole coral communities.
The effects of changes in sea level	Coral reefs need sunlight, but as sea levels rise this is reduced by the deeper water above them. Sea levels have risen by 10–25 cm over the past century, and are forecast to rise 15–95 cm over the next. Quick-growing species can keep pace with sea level rises but slow-growing species need shallow water.
Rise in sea temperatures	Sea temperatures may be increasing by about 1–2 °C per century. Coral reefs can only grow within a certain temperature range. Above this, corals deteriorate and may die. This is known as *coral bleaching*.

B Natural threats to coral reefs

Coral reefs – a magnet for tourism

Tourism is the world's fastest growing industry. Coral reefs are a resource that attracts large numbers of tourists from around the world to places like the Caribbean. One hundred million visitors flock to the Caribbean every year, earning 40 per cent of the region's Gross National Product (GNP).

The sheer beauty of coral reefs is just one of the attractions for the visitor. Scuba diving is increasingly popular and allows the tourist to get a close look at this diverse ecosystem and its varied marine life. Unfortunately, it also directly affects the health of coral reefs.

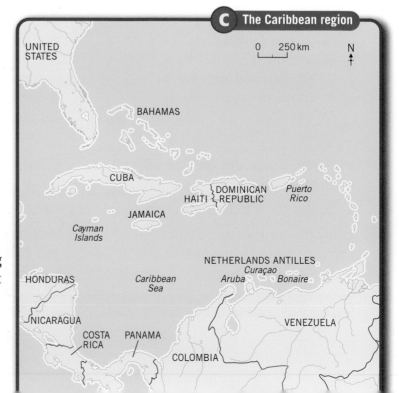

C The Caribbean region

0   250 km   N

UNITED STATES

BAHAMAS

CUBA

CAYMAN Islands

JAMAICA

HAITI DOMINICAN REPUBLIC

Puerto Rico

HONDURAS

Caribbean Sea

NETHERLANDS ANTILLES
Curaçao
Aruba   Bonaire

NICARAGUA

VENEZUELA

COSTA RICA   PANAMA

COLOMBIA

Tourist activity		Damage caused
Scuba diving		Divers can damage the delicate coral reef ecosystems.
Snorkelling		Inexperienced snorkellers can trample coral with their flippers, by getting too close or resting on the reef. They often do not realise the damage they cause.
Boat trips		Cruises taking visitors out to the reefs are often careless where they drop anchor.
Boat trips		The water movement caused by boats travelling too fast or too close damages coral reefs.
Boat hire		Tourists do not know the local waters and can run aground on a reef.

D Direct impacts of tourism on coral reef ecosystems

Curaçao

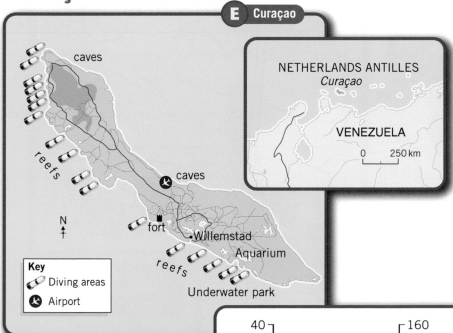

E Curaçao

NETHERLANDS ANTILLES
Curaçao

VENEZUELA

0   250 km

caves

reefs

N

caves

fort

Willemstad

Aquarium

reefs

Underwater park

Key
- Diving areas
- Airport

Curaçao may be a tourist paradise, but it is a conservationist's nightmare. Today, few tourists in the Caribbean stop here. But if tourist development is not carefully managed it could become yet another tropical island swamped by hotel chains and wealthy western tourists.

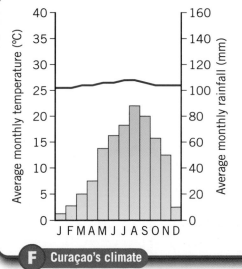

F Curaçao's climate

Activities

1. Imagine that you are planning a holiday to Curaçao. Use the information on these pages and an atlas to help you plan your trip.

   a Describe the location of Curaçao.

   b Use climate graph **F** to write a short description of the climate of Curaçao. Suggest a good time of year to visit the island.

   c Study map **E**. Which part of the island do you think has more tourist development – the east or west coast? Explain your reasons.

   d Write a postcard home describing your time on the island: www.heinemann.co.uk/hotlinks will help you add more detail.

2. Table **D** shows the direct impacts tourists can have on coral reefs. Use the following phrases to produce a similar table showing the indirect impacts tourism may have on coral reefs.
   - Solid waste disposal from cruise boats
   - Pollution from coastal tourism development
   - Overfishing the reefs to feed the increasing number of tourists
   - Local rural people looking for work in the tourist industry set up squatter camps on the coast.

3. Tourists and boat crews damage coral reefs mainly through ignorance. Design an information sheet to explain to tourists visiting Curaçao how and why they should use the reefs carefully. Suggest where it should be displayed.

4. Use the website at www.heinemann.co.uk/hotlinks (insert code 5171P) to find out more about Curaçao.

Review and reflect

In this unit you have studied ecosystems, a variety of natural resources and the way people use and misuse them. You have learned that people often have different views and attitudes about resource issues and how to solve them for the future. You may have discovered that, even within your class, students' opinions about resources and the environment can be very different.

The overexploitation of any resource is not a responsible way to manage our global ecosystems. As you have seen in this unit, overfishing of our oceans and seas is creating social, economic and environmental problems. These problems are repeated where any natural resource is being exploited, not just for the current generation but for those in the future too. If we are to show consideration for future generations, then we need to manage natural resources in a more sustainable way.

A Our future environment?

B The kids were thrilled after finding sandcastle aids already on the beach.

We caught him in polluted water C

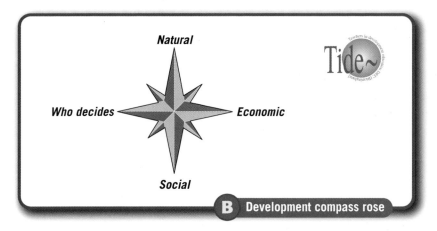

B Development compass rose

Activities

1 a Work in pairs or small groups. Look back through this unit and make a list in rough of all the resource and environmental issues you have studied. Write down:

- what the issue is
- where the examples you studied are located
- a few key points about the issue, for example the problem and solution.

b Stick an outline map of the world in the centre of a large piece of paper. Locate all the issues on the map, then neatly annotate (label) on the details about each.

c Discuss which issues:

- have already had an effect on your lives
- might affect young people in other parts of the world
- might affect young people in future.

d Find a way of showing your ideas on your map.

2 Choose one resource or environmental issue from this unit to think about in depth.

a Make a copy of the development compass rose **B** in the centre of a large piece of paper.

b In pairs, discuss the issue, then write around the outside which problems or changes are:

- **N**atural – to do with ecosystems
- **E**conomic – to do with jobs and money
- **S**ocial – to do with people and the way they live
- **W**ho decides – the people who make decisions.

3 Choose one of the cartoons on page 128 that shows a negative global future.

a In pairs, discuss what you think it is saying about the future.

b Each design your own cartoon to show a positive future, or the future you would prefer.

c Discuss the main differences between the cartoons.

d Finally, write a summary of your ideas – make sure you include some of these key words from this unit:

- sustainable
- resource
- conservation
- ecosystem.

8 Crime and the local community

A Violence at anti-Capitalism protests, London, 2000

B ITV's The Bill, a popular image of the police

C Peaceful protests in Seattle, USA, 2000

D Graffiti on a train

E CCTV in Oxford

WARNING!
CLOSED CIRCUIT TELEVISION
WITH VIDEO RECORDING
OPERATES ON THESE PREMISES
Chris Lewis
SECURITY SERVICES
☎ 01865 744777

Learn about

Crime happens all over the world – in cities, in towns and in the countryside. Some types of crime affect people much more than others. Views on different types of crime vary from person to person. This unit looks at patterns of criminal activity within local areas. You are going to investigate:

◎ what crime is and how it is caused

◎ what people feel about crime

◎ how crime varies locally and nationally

◎ how the problem of crime might be solved.

What is crime?

A **crime** is any action or offence that is punishable by law. Crimes include murder, burglary, assault, robbery, sexual assault, shoplifting, joyriding, blackmail and fraud.

Reported crimes in the UK are falling: according to the 2000 British Crime Survey, burglaries were down by 20 per cent and car thefts had fallen by 15 per cent since 1998. However, the rate of crime is still high.

- Shoplifting in the UK totalled £1.4 billion in 1996–1997.
- More than one in twenty British homes is burgled every year.
- Half of all violence by strangers is committed by people who have been drinking.

Is all crime recorded?

Information about crime can be obtained from official police records, court records, newspaper reports, crime surveys, the Internet and questionnaires. However, the data is not always reliable.

Most information about crime comes from official police data, but only about a quarter of all crime is reported to the police.

- Some crimes are not reported because people think they are trivial. An example is speeding, although it may lead to accidents and death.
- The young and people from ethnic minorities may be unhappy with the service they get from the police.
- Many violent assaults, sexual attacks and other crimes are not reported because the victim knows the attacker.

- About 80 per cent of criminals are male.
- Babies under the age of one year are at more risk of being murdered than any other age group.

What are the causes of crime?

- Poverty and unemployment may cause people to turn to crime.
- Young people are the most likely to be involved in crime. However, the proportion of young criminals is going down.
- In rich societies there is more to steal.
- Drug use and the costs of buying illegal drugs have led some people into crime.

Activities

1. Add your own definition of the word *crime* to your word bank.

2. In a group of three or four, list all the different types of crime that you can think of. Look at photos **A** to **E** to get you started.

3. Classify the crimes on your list into categories.

   a. Group together similar types of crime.

   b. Group the crimes according to how serious you think they are.

4. Investigate how crime is portrayed in the media.

   a. Make a list of TV entertainment programmes that involve crime.

      i. What sorts of crimes do they show?

      ii. Where do they show crimes taking place?

      iii. How realistic do you think they are?

   b. Watch the TV national news and read the local newspaper for two weeks.

      i. What crimes have been reported on the national news?

      ii. Where do they take place?

      iii. How similar are they to crimes reported for your home area?

      iv. What does this show about the type of crime reported, and how representative it is?

What do people feel about crime?

Getting Technical ▼

- **Burglary:** entering a building illegally in order to commit a crime
- **Robbery:** stealing from somebody by threatening to use, or using, violence
- **Vehicle theft:** stealing, or trying to steal, a car, van, motorbike, etc. or a part of that vehicle
- **Fraud:** using trickery or cheating to steal something

Are people afraid of crime?

A survey was published in 1996 on fear of crime in urban and rural areas. The results were rather surprising (see table **A**).

A Percentages of people who feel very worried about some types of crimes

	London				England and Wales			
	Males aged 16–59	Males aged 60 and over	Females aged 16–59	Females aged 60 and over	Males aged 16–59	Males aged 60 and over	Females aged 16–59	Females aged 60 and over
Burglary	23	21	28	23	18	18	26	25
Mugging	15	19	26	26	12	13	26	26
Theft of car	24	17	23	10	24	19	27	23
Racial attack	10	9	18	11	6	4	12	7

The survey showed that fear of crime is common in urban areas. This is partly because older people feel afraid of large numbers of younger people, and also because most crime takes place in urban areas.

However, the fear of crime in rural areas is also high, although the number of crimes committed is quite low. The detection rate is relatively low – 26 per cent of all rural crimes are solved. In England and Wales as a whole the detection rate is 29 per cent.

People in country areas fear crime for a number of reasons. The elderly, in particular, may be afraid because they are isolated. Compared with 30 years ago, people in rural areas:

- are more nervous and less trusting
- are more fearful of crime
- have fewer police officers nearby to protect them
- are more aware that national levels of most crimes have increased.

Table **B** shows the reported crime in Wiltshire, a mainly rural area in southern England. You can see the figures for Greater London in table **C**.

Type of crime	Number of offences	% of all crimes
Theft	16 746	44
Burglary	5 718	15
Criminal damage	7 151	19
Violence	4 519	12
Fraud and forgery	2 086	5
Robbery	258	1
Drug offences	1 172	3
Other offences	811	2
Total crimes	38 461	
Total population	593 300	

B Reported crime in Wiltshire, 1999–2000

Type of crime	Number of offences	% of all crimes
Theft	426 235	41
Burglary	129 145	13
Criminal damage	151 590	14
Violence	156 880	15
Fraud and forgery	105 150	10
Robbery	36 317	3
Drug offences	26 233	3
Other offences	20 497	2
Total crimes	1 052 047	
Total population	7 285 000	

C Reported crime in London, 1999–2000

Activities

1 Study the data in table **A**.
   a Draw a multiple bar graph to show how different groups of people fear theft of a car in London and in the rest of England and Wales. ①②③
   b Describe what your graph shows, then try to explain your findings. 📖

2 Study the data in table **B**.
   a Draw a pie graph to show reported crime in Wiltshire in 1999–2000. ①②③
   b Describe what your graph shows. The writing frame below will help you. 📖

> In Wiltshire in 1999-2000, the total number of reported crimes was … The pie graph shows that some crimes made up a large percentage of the total. These include … Other crimes … I also notice that … Overall, the pie graph tells me …

3 Compare the graphs you have drawn. ①②③
   a Which was the quickest or easiest to draw?
   b Which shows the information in the clearest way?

4 Look at the data in tables **B** and **C**. Compare the crime rates in the two areas. Remember that the population of Greater London is about twelve times as big as that of Wiltshire. Do you think that people in rural areas are too worried about crime?

How to ...

... draw a multiple bar graph

A multiple bar graph is good for showing more than one set of data, divided into groups and categories, such as people worried about car theft in London and in England and Wales.

1 Draw two axes on graph paper. The vertical (*y*) axis has a numerical scale – percentage of people worried. The horizontal (*x*) axis shows the groups of people.

2 Plot the data for people worried about car theft in London. The bars for males have been done for you. Add two bars for females.

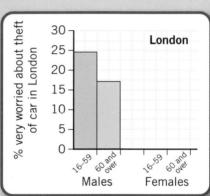

3 Draw a similar multiple bar graph for England and Wales.

How to ...

... draw a pie graph

A pie graph divides up a circle like slices of a pie. It is a good way to show percentages of something, like the different crimes committed in Wiltshire.

1 Use a calculator to turn all the percentages into degrees. For example, theft: 44% or $\frac{44}{100}$:
   $$\frac{44}{100} \times 360° \text{ (degrees in a circle)} = 158°$$

2 Use compasses to draw a circle. Use a protractor to mark 158°.

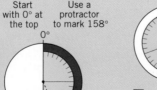

3 Mark the first segment, then repeat for the other crimes.

4 Add a key and title to your graph.

Where do people expect crime to happen?

Case Study: Crime in Oxford

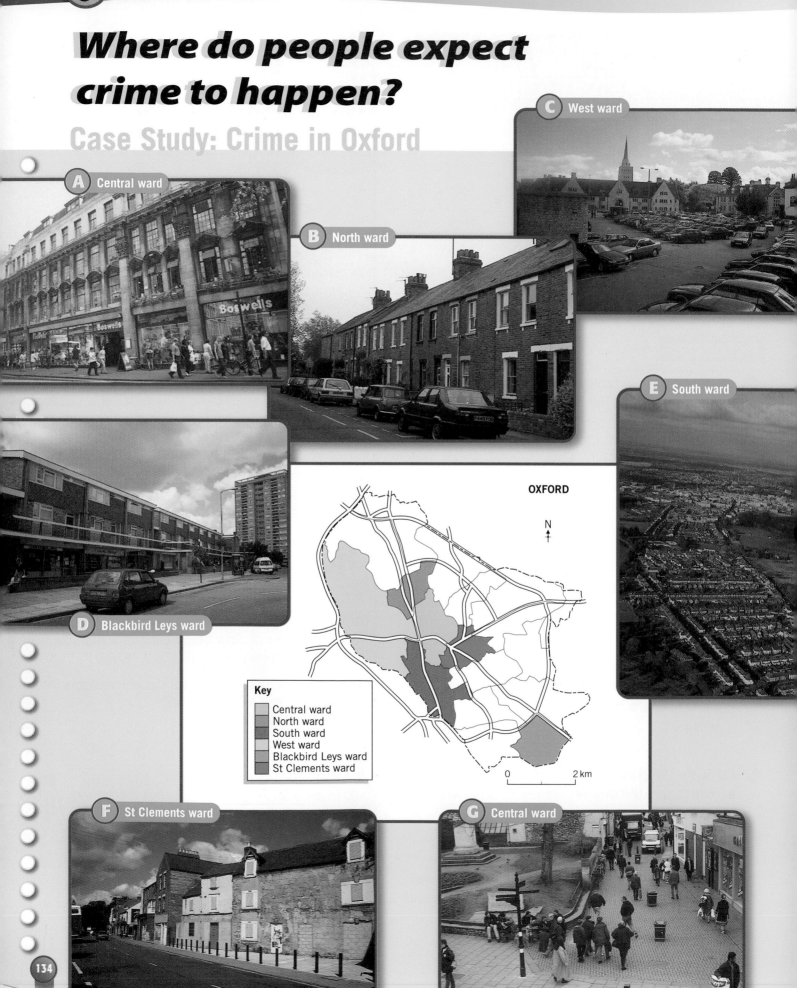

A Central ward

B North ward

C West ward

D Blackbird Leys ward

E South ward

F St Clements ward

G Central ward

OXFORD

N

Key
- Central ward
- North ward
- South ward
- West ward
- Blackbird Leys ward
- St Clements ward

0   2 km

H Barton, part of Headington ward

Oxford is a medium-sized city with a population of about 115 000 people. It is a good place to study crime because levels of violence and crime are not particularly high. Photographs **A** to **H** show different areas of Oxford. The activities will help you think about your perceptions of crime. Table **I** shows the crime figures for the different **wards**, or districts, of Oxford.

Ward	All crime
Oxford total	25 678
Central	4 671
St Clements	2 185
Quarry Ward	2 005
North	1 706
Blackbird Leys	1 467
Iffley	1 318
Headington Ward	1 179
East Ward	1 093
Temple Cowley	1 078
Wolvercote	978
Marston Ward	957
South	885
Littlemore	811
West	775
Wood Farm	758
Cherwell	752
Marston Parish	495
Risinghurst	295

I Crime figures for Oxford by ward, 1998

Data provided by the Thames Valley Police

Activities

1 Study photographs **A** to **H**.

  a Copy the table below. Grade each picture on a scale of 1–5, where 1 is safe and 5 is unsafe.

  b Write down what you find most comforting or most uncomfortable about the photographs.

Photo	Score	Reason
A		

2 Put your results together with those of the rest of the class.

  ◎ Which areas do people think are most safe and least safe?

  ◎ Is there any variation between the results for girls and boys?

3 Now compare the results from your class's survey with those in **I**.

  a List the areas in order, according to your survey.

  b Now compare them to the order produced by the Thames Valley Police.

   i How do they compare?

   ii Can you think of reasons for any differences that you have noted?

4 **Extension**

Take photographs of your local area which show contrasting images. Show them to a friend or family member and ask them to score the images as you did for activity **1**. Make a short presentation about people's impression of crime. You could use a digital camera and presentation software. (ICT)

Mapping crime in Oxford

Oxford has a mix of population groups, wide variations in standards of living and a fairly low unemployment rate. Housing conditions range from wealthy areas in North Oxford to the housing estates at Barton and Blackbird Leys on the edge of the city. However, there is a considerable mix of housing in all areas. Oxford has a mix of residential and recreational areas, with some industrial and commercial land-uses. Map **A** shows the overall pattern of crime in Oxford.

Patterns of crime in Oxford – are they changing?

Burglary in Oxford is a widespread problem, though it is concentrated in east and south Oxford. In particular, the area bordering the Cowley Road has over 10 per cent of all recorded burglaries (see **B**). You might expect that higher income areas would have more burglaries, because of more detached housing, better screening by trees, and richer pickings for burglars. In reality, most burglaries take place quite close to the offender's home or in places that the offender knows well. The burglaries in central Oxford may be because criminals know this area well.

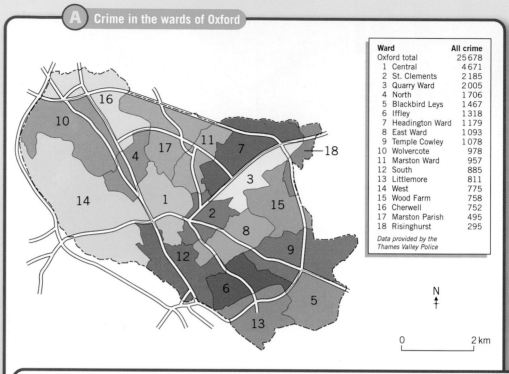

A Crime in the wards of Oxford

Ward	All crime
Oxford total	25 678
1 Central	4 671
2 St. Clements	2 185
3 Quarry Ward	2 005
4 North	1 706
5 Blackbird Leys	1 467
6 Iffley	1 318
7 Headington Ward	1 179
8 East Ward	1 093
9 Temple Cowley	1 078
10 Wolvercote	978
11 Marston Ward	957
12 South	885
13 Littlemore	811
14 West	775
15 Wood Farm	758
16 Cherwell	752
17 Marston Parish	495
18 Risinghurst	295

Data provided by the Thames Valley Police

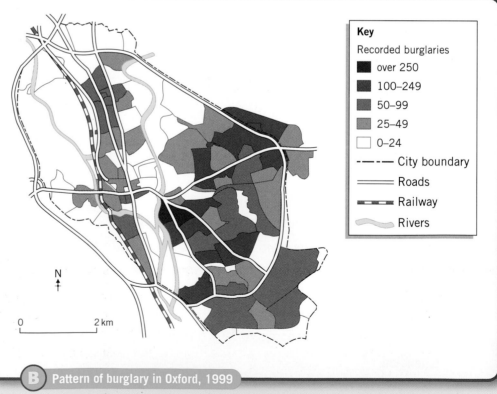

Key

Recorded burglaries

■	over 250
■	100–249
■	50–99
■	25–49
□	0–24
–·–·–	City boundary
═══	Roads
▬▬▬	Railway
〰〰	Rivers

B Pattern of burglary in Oxford, 1999

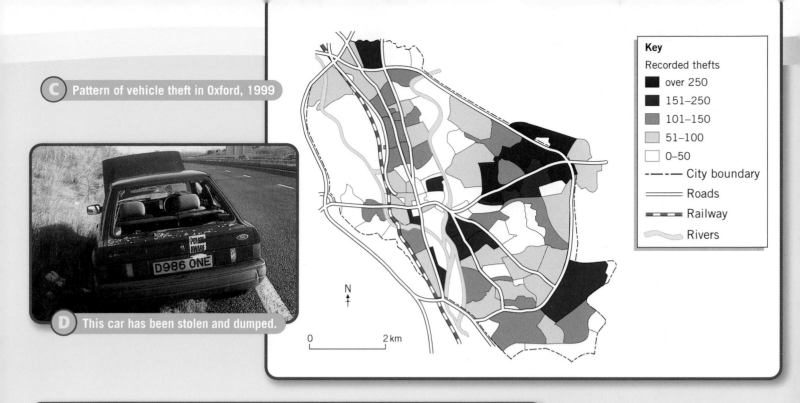

C Pattern of vehicle theft in Oxford, 1999

Key
Recorded thefts
- ■ over 250
- ■ 151–250
- ▨ 101–150
- ▨ 51–100
- □ 0–50
- —·— City boundary
- ═══ Roads
- ▬▬ Railway
- ∿ Rivers

D This car has been stolen and dumped.

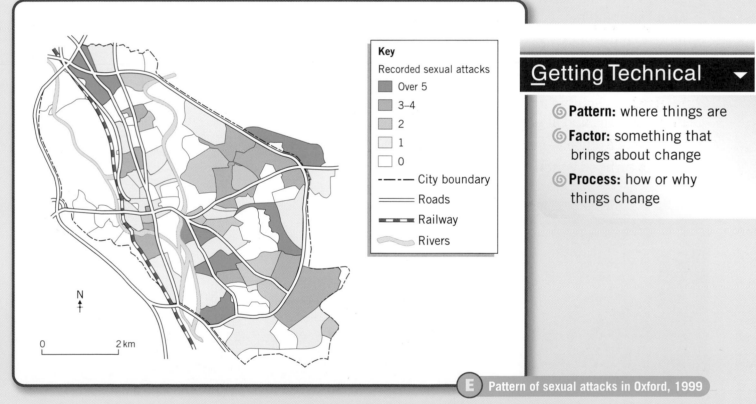

Key
Recorded sexual attacks
- ■ Over 5
- ▨ 3–4
- ▨ 2
- ▨ 1
- □ 0
- —·— City boundary
- ═══ Roads
- ▬▬ Railway
- ∿ Rivers

Getting Technical ▼

- **Pattern:** where things are
- **Factor:** something that brings about change
- **Process:** how or why things change

E Pattern of sexual attacks in Oxford, 1999

Vehicle theft (see **C**) is widespread in Oxford and accounts for over 25 per cent of all recorded crimes. The **pattern** is related to the location of car parks, hospitals, centres of employment and areas where joyriding happens, such as Blackbird Leys. Car crime data is reliable since car insurance claims have to be reported to the police.

Sexual attacks provide the most **dispersed** pattern of crime in Oxford (map **E**). Two **factors** help explain the pattern: the location of vulnerable groups (especially young, single women, such as students) and the location of dangerous areas (with lots of cover for attackers).

Other forms of crime produce a more predictable distribution. Shoplifting is most common where there are many shops. Most crimes are concentrated in the city centre, despite the closed-circuit TV (CCTV) there.

Fighting crime

The risk of burglary increases with poor security, carelessness, and the presence of flats, maisonettes and single-adult households. Over half of all burglaries happen during the evening or night. A further 10 per cent occur when the victim is away for the weekend or on holiday. Although stolen property is rarely recovered, most households are insured against burglary. Because most burglaries are reported to insurance companies, the police statistics for burglary are more accurate than for many other crimes.

Knowing where crime takes place helps the authorities to lower crime levels. Crime prevention methods in Oxford include:

- a new radio-link between shops to warn about shoplifters
- increased use of CCTV
- the removal of strong drinks from city centre off-licences
- better street lighting to improve safety in the evening and at night
- more police officers on the beat
- Neighbourhood Watch schemes.

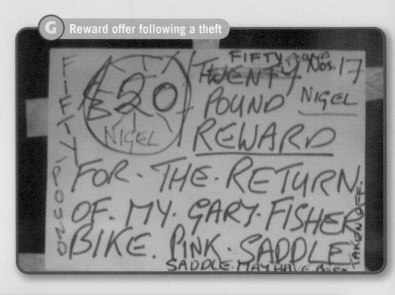

G Reward offer following a theft

F An underpass in Oxford

E Neighbourhood watch scheme

I Aerial photo of Marston, an area of Oxford

H Security alarms on recent housing developments

How to ...

... plot a density map of crime in Oxford

Density maps are sometimes called **choropleth** maps. Map **B** on page 136 is a choropleth map.

1 Decide on six groups, e.g. 0–799, 800–1599, 1600–2399, 2400–3199, 3200–3999 and over 4000 crimes per year.

2 Choose six colours – similar colours or shades are best. Shade the areas with the most crimes with the darkest shade, and shade the areas with the smallest amount of crime with the lightest shade.

Activities

1 a Maps **B**, **C** and **D** on pages 136–137 are **density maps**. On a copy of map **A**, plot a density map to show the distribution of total crime in Oxford. (123)

   b Describe and explain the distribution. You could do this by labelling key points from the text around your map.

2 The aerial photograph in **I** shows Marston, an area of Oxford.

   a Look back at the information on pages 136 and 137. Suggest what types of crime might be found in the area shown in **I**.

   b Suggest ways in which the area could be made safer. You could label your suggestions around a copy or sketch of **I**. Remember to explain your ideas.

3 The Thames Valley Police website is listed at: www.heinemann.co.uk/hotlinks (insert code 5171P). Use it to investigate the enquiry question:

   What are the Thames Valley Police doing to reduce crime, disorder and fear in the Thames Valley region? (ICT)

4 Look at photo **F**. How could this area be made safer?

5 The Thames Valley Police website also has a list of **frequently asked questions (FAQs)** about young people and the law. It tells you about your rights, and also what happens to those who commit an offence.

   Investigate the Thames Valley Police website or the site of your local force. Use the information to design a leaflet or poster to tell young people about how the law affects them. (ICT) 📖

6 a In groups of three or four, make a list of five questions you might ask about crime.

   b Use the Internet to investigate your questions. The websites listed at www.heinemann.co.uk/hotlinks (insert code 5171P) contain information about crime. (ICT)

Patterns of crime nationwide

Activities

1 Use map **A** and an atlas to investigate the pattern of crime in England and Wales.

a Make lists of areas with the highest and lowest rates of crime. You could set your work out in a table like this:

High crime areas	Low crime areas
London	

b Discuss with a partner which sorts of areas have high crime rates and which have low crime rates. A population density map might help you here. Write notes about the main pattern you notice on the map.

c Finally, look for anything surprising on the map. For example, are there any places you would expect to have a high rate of crime, but which do not?

2 a Discuss with your partner what factors or reasons might explain the pattern you have found. Your work on the rest of this unit should help you with this.

b Share your ideas with another pair or the whole class – try to agree a short list of possible reasons for differences in crime rates.

3 You are now ready to write a short report on patterns of crime in the UK. The writing frame below may help you:

> I am going to describe the main features of ...
>
> One of the main things I noticed ...
>
> Some areas ...
>
> However, ...
>
> The main factors which explain this pattern ...
>
> To summarise ...

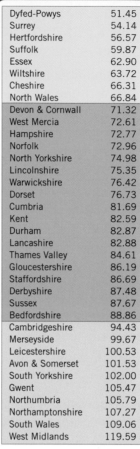
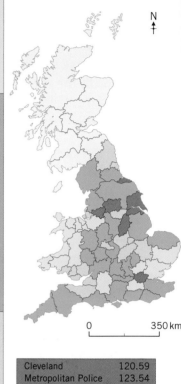

Dyfed-Powys	51.45
Surrey	54.14
Hertfordshire	56.57
Suffolk	59.87
Essex	62.90
Wiltshire	63.72
Cheshire	66.31
North Wales	66.84
Devon & Cornwall	71.32
West Mercia	72.61
Hampshire	72.77
Norfolk	72.96
North Yorkshire	74.98
Lincolnshire	75.35
Warwickshire	76.42
Dorset	76.73
Cumbria	81.69
Kent	82.59
Durham	82.87
Lancashire	82.88
Thames Valley	84.61
Gloucestershire	86.19
Staffordshire	86.69
Derbyshire	87.48
Sussex	87.67
Bedfordshire	88.86
Cambridgeshire	94.43
Merseyside	99.67
Leicestershire	100.53
Avon & Somerset	101.53
South Yorkshire	102.00
Gwent	105.47
Northumbria	105.79
Northamptonshire	107.27
South Wales	109.06
West Midlands	119.59

Cleveland	120.59
Metropolitan Police	123.54
West Yorkshire	129.76
Nottinghamshire	131.04
Greater Manchester	140.93
Humberside	147.72

A Reported crimes per thousand people in England and Wales

help!

Remember, good detectives:

- ☸ start with a theory about the general pattern
- ☸ give examples to support their argument
- ☸ may give some examples which don't exactly fit the pattern
- ☸ give factors which explain the findings.

Review and reflect

Things you have learned about	Pages	Examples	Geography skills	Key skills
What is crime?	131	UK		
What are the causes of crime?	131	UK		
What do people feel about crime?	132, 133	Wiltshire, London, UK		
Where do people expect crime to happen?	134, 135	Oxford		
Mapping crime in Oxford	136, 137	Oxford		
Patterns of crime nationwide	140	UK		

Activities

1 Make a large copy of the table above.

a Complete the fourth column, which reminds you what geographical skills you have used. For example, you may have drawn a map, summarised data, looked at photographs and drawn conclusions, described a pattern and suggested reasons to explain a pattern.

b Think again about how you did the activities. You should be able to come up with a list of key skills to put in the fifth column.

2 Look back through this unit to check that you know the meaning of the key words in **bold**. Use them to update your geography word bank.

3 **Extension**

Conduct a class debate on an issue in crime that your class finds interesting. Use what you have learned about crime from this chapter, but think especially about your local area. For example, you may wish to argue that:

Young people are not that bad – despite the statistics

or discuss some other aspects of crime that affect young people. You could ask the Police Community Liaison Officer or Schools Liaison Officer to come along and give a presentation to the class and listen to your points of view.

help!

Your key skills may include:

- communication (language)
- numeracy
- ICT
- working with others
- improving your own learning.

Glossary

Adaptations   special features developed by plants to help them survive in an environment, e.g. extreme hot and dry conditions.

Altitude   height of the land above sea level.

Arch   a natural rock bridge formed when the sea erodes through a headland.

Arterial roads   main roads which link important towns.

Atmosphere   the layer of gases surrounding the Earth.

Audience   the people who use a shopping area.

Bedding planes   horizontal cracks between layers of rock.

Calcium carbonate   the chemical formula for limestone rock.

Cave   a hole beneath the surface or in a cliff formed by the action of water.

Cavern   a large cave formed by meltwater.

Chalk   a hard, white sedimentary rock made up of the skeletons of millions of tiny sea animals.

Charcoal   a raw material made of partly burnt wood. It can be used instead of coal to make iron.

Choropleth map   a map using density shading for particular groups. It is also known as a **density map**.

Cirrus   high-level cloud formed of ice crystals.

Clay   a soft, fine sedimentary rock.

Clints   the surface 'slabs' of rock on a limestone pavement.

Community   a group of plants and animals living closely together.

Conflict   where groups of people have different ideas about how an area should be used. These conflicts can be shown on a conflict matrix.

Convection rain   heavy rain formed by the cooling of moist air which has risen from the heated ground or sea.

Crime   an action that breaks the law.

Crude oil   petroleum in its natural liquid state as it emerges from the ground, before refining.

Cumulonimbus   very tall storm clouds formed when air rises very quickly.

Cumulus   heaped up masses of cloud with bumpy tops.

Density map   see **choropleth map**.

Deposition   when a river or the sea dumps or **deposits** what it is carrying.

Discharge   the volume of water which passes through a river at one point in time, measured in cubic metres per second.

Dispersed   scattered.

Drought   a period of low rainfall, often over many years.

Dry valleys   valleys formed on permeable rock after the Ice Age; water now flows underneath them because the rocks have thawed out.

Economic development   the success of an area or country at producing useful goods.

Equatorial   a type of climate found near the Equator.

Evapotranspiration   the total loss of water by evaporation from the soil and other surfaces plus water released from plants.

Extensive ranching   cattle farming in which there are only a few cattle per hectare.

Feeder roads   small roads which link into main roads.

Food chain   a cycle that begins with green plants that take their energy from sunlight, continuing with organisms that eat these plants, to other organisms that consume the plant-eating organisms, then to decomposers that break down the dead bodies of those organisms so that they can be used as soil nutrients by plants, starting the cycle again.

Forecast   a weather forecast is a prediction of future weather using scientific evidence.

Frequently asked questions (FAQs)   the part of a website that provides answers to the questions that people ask most often.

Frontal rain   precipitation caused when warm air is forced to rise over cooler air.

Gradient   slope.

Granite   a very hard igneous rock made of crystals of minerals.

Grykes   gaps between blocks of stone on a *limestone pavement*.

Headlands   hard rocks which are left jutting out into the sea, often as cliffs.

Herbicides   chemicals put onto the land to control weeds.

Hierarchy   a series of geographical features that build up: for example, a small village, a market town, a large town, a city.

Honeypot   a place, often part of a larger tourist area, that attracts large numbers of tourists.

Humidity the amount of water vapour held in the air. When this is high the weather is **humid**.

Hydro-electric power a way of generating electricity by using the force of water to turn a turbine.

Hydrological cycle a never-ending circulation of water: water evaporates from the sea and land, rises and condenses to form clouds. It then falls back to Earth as precipitation.

Ice ages periods of time when the land surface was covered in ice due to low temperatures. The last Ice Age in the UK was between 19 000 and 10 000 years ago.

Intensive farming in which a lot of crop is produced per hectare.

Isotherm a line on a map that joins places with the same temperature.

Joints vertical cracks in rock.

Latitude distance north or south of the Equator measured in degrees.

Layer shading a method of showing the height of land using a series of colours.

Limestone a sedimentary rock formed from calcium and the carbon remains of sea creatures.

Limestone pavements limestone exposed at the surface to reveal *clints* and *grykes*.

Limestone scars vertical rock faces that are exposed.

Longshore drift the transport of material along a beach. It happens when waves hit the beach at an angle.

Lowland land between 0 and 100 metres above sea level, usually fairly flat.

Marble a hard metamorphic rock.

Meteorologist a scientist who studies the weather.

Ocean current a flow of warm or cold water.

Ozone layer the layer of the upper atmosphere, from about 12 to 50 kilometres above the Earth's surface, that protects the Earth from harmful radiation from the Sun.

Photosynthesis green plants use the energy of sunlight to convert carbon dioxide and water into energy which they use for growth. At the same time they release oxygen into the air.

Pillars formed when stalactites and stalagmites join together.

Plateau a high flat-topped hill or hilly area.

Porous rocks with tiny holes in them which hold water are porous.

Prevailing winds the winds which blow most frequently over an area, described by the compass direction from which they come.

Primary productivity the rate at which green plants, store energy as carbohydrates to be consumed by other organisms.

Refined oil oil in a form that can be used in, for example, homes and cars. It is made by removing the impurities from crude oil.

Relief rain precipitation caused when air is forced to rise over hills and mountains.

Resurgence where water emerges at the surface.

Retail goods goods bought by consumers, often in shops.

Revetment a barrier placed along the foot of a cliff or sea wall to break the power of the waves before they reach the coast.

Savanna an area of tropical grassland with tall grasses and the occasional tree.

Selva rainforest.

Sink a place where water disappears underground as it reaches permeable rock.

Spit a long beach formed by longshore drift. Spits often stretch across the mouths of rivers or where the coast suddenly changes direction.

Spring a place where water reaches the surface, for example after passing through permeable rock.

Stack the remains of collapsed arches left when a cliffline retreats.

Stalactites icicle-shaped deposits of calcium carbonate hanging from a cave roof.

Stalagmites deposits of calcium carbonate which build up on a cave floor.

Stratus low clouds forming a layer or 'sheet' across the sky.

Sustainability the wise use of resources today, so that people in the future can still use them. Resources used in this way are **sustainable**.

Swallow hole a funnel shaped hole which leads underground.

Temperature how hot or cold a place is.

Transport carry; for example, rock fragments that have been eroded are removed or transported by the sea, wind, ice or rivers.

Upland land above 100 metres above sea level, usually hills or mountains.

Velocity the speed of a river, calculated in metres per second.

Ward a small area (political division) in a town or city.

Water vapour water when it is a gas.

Weathering the breakdown of rocks due to exposure to air, moisture and plants and animals.

Index